303 TRICKY CHESS PUZZLES

ABOUT THE AUTHORS

FRED WILSON

Fred Wilson is among the finest chess teachers and authors. He has authored *202 Surprising Mates, 303 Tricky Chess Tactics, 303 Tricky Checkmates* and *202 Checkmates for Children*, all with Bruce Alberston for Cardoza Publishing. He has also written three other books: *A Picture History of Chess* and *101 Questions on How to Play Chess*. He is also the owner of Fred Wilson Chess Books in New York City.

BRUCE ALBERSTON

Bruce Alberston is a well-known chess trainer and teacher in the New York city area and has recently written and narrated the best-selling CD-ROM, *Quick Kills on the Chessboard*, and collaborated with Fred Wilson on *202 Surprising Mates, 303 Tricky Chess Tactics, 303 Tricky Checkmates* and *202 Checkmates for Children*.

303
TRICKY CHESS
PUZZLES

Fred Wilson & Bruce Alberston

CARDOZA PUBLISHING

Cardoza Publishing is the foremost gaming publisher in the world, with a library of over 100 up-to-date and easy-to-read books and strategies. These authoritative works are written by the top experts in their fields and, with more than 7,500,000 books in print, represent the best-selling and most popular gaming books anywhere.

FIRST EDITION

Copyright © 2004 by Fred Wilson & Bruce Alberston
- All Rights Reserved -

Library of Congress Catalog Card No: 2004101422
ISBN: 1-58042-144-X

Visit our web site (www.cardozapub.com)
or write us for a full list of books and computer strategies.

CARDOZA PUBLISHING
P.O. Box 1500, Cooper Station, New York, NY 10276
Phone (800)577-WINS
email: cardozapub@aol.com
www.cardozapub.com

TABLE OF CONTENTS

INTRODUCTION

Get ready to have a lot of fun and improve your chess skills at the same time! We've put together 303 fascinating puzzles; your challenge is to find the decisive move which gets you material superiority, leads to a forced mate, or simply allows you to survive!

You'll have to employ your entire arsenal of tactics to solve these dilemmas, including lesser-known tactics—such as survival, trapping and promotion. As in our earlier books—*303 Tricky Checkmates* and *303 Tricky Chess Tactics*—we present two large, clear diagrams per page, making it easier for you to calculate and visualize the possibilities. More than one-third of the positions are "Black to Move," to give you practice at looking at the game from Black's perspective.

We encourage you to go through this book more than once—indeed, several times—until you become quite comfortable at solving all the positions. Additionally, we suggest that before commencing any serious chess play, especially a tournament game, you solve at least five puzzles from each chapter as a tactical warm-up to ready you for battle.

More than anything else, this is a practical workbook and great training tool that will help you improve your tactics and your game. Let's get started!

OVERVIEW

By some ardent enthusiasts chess has been elevated into a science or an art. It is neither; but its principal characteristic seems to be what human nature mostly delights in—a fight.

—Emanuel Lasker

If Emanuel Lasker, one of the strongest players of all time, believed that chess is a fight, perhaps he was on to something. In a chess fight, just as in a boxing match, you must be constantly alert for tactical opportunities, while also trying to create your own. And you must develop this sense of tactical alertness in both attack and defense. To quote Fischer: "You've [not only] got to know when to punch, but how to duck." After all, when you play chess you have an opponent who is actively trying to thwart you. No matter how clever your overall strategy has been, or how worn down he seems, it won't mean a thing if you're the one who overlooks a tactical knockout!

You'd think that chess players would consider solving tactical puzzles to be a good idea—a no-brainer, even. But so many players don't! Collectively, we have over fifty years experience as chess teachers, and in that time, we have found that the single greatest impediment to chess improvement is the amateur's reluctance to study tactics.

At the top of each diagram, we've provided hints that should be especially helpful in Chapters 2 and 3. Also, we have often included written explanations with the solutions at the end of the book to help clarify difficult variations and/or concepts.

We have devoted Chapter 1, a full third of the book, to finding forced checkmates. Contrary to the idea that you should occupy most of your study time solving material winning problems, we have observed that checkmating opportunities are missed all the time! In the following position, Peter J. Tamburro, Jr., our good friend and fellow teacher and author, has lured Black's king to f6 by capturing the g7 pawn on his last move. As this was a five-minute internet game, Black certainly thought Peter had blundered by allowing his rook and knight to be forked by Black's king. What did he overlook?

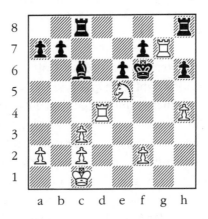

After **1. Rxf7+ Kxe5; 2. f4#!**, he found out that Peter really knows his tactics.

In the next position, White believed that if he could just achieve the move **e4,** attacking Black's queen and allowing his undeveloped queenside pieces to get out, he might be able to save the game. However, it was Black's move, so how did he put a swift end to White's suffering?

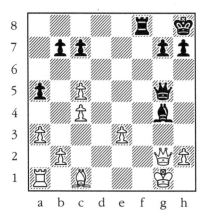

After the startling **1...Bh3!**, White cannot prevent mate next move if **2. Qxg5 Rf1#.**

Having conducted a blistering sacrificial attack, IM Pedzich now had to decide whether to settle for a draw by perpetual check against IM Murdzia at Swidnica, 1999. You can all calculate that **1. Qg6+ Kg8; 2. Qf7+ Kh7 3. Qg6+** gives White a perpetual check (see below), but did Pedzich find something better?

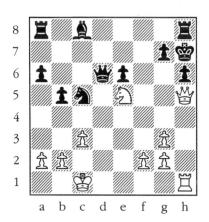

Hopefully, you also found that after **1. Qg6+ Kg8; 2. Qf7+ Kh7,** White has **3. Rxh6+! Kxh6; 4. Qg6#** to finish up a well-played attack.

Chapter 2 deals with winning material and the standard tactics you need to master in order to do so. While we are certain you know common tactics such as pins, forks, skewers, and discoveries, we would like you to play through the following beautiful and oddly little-known game in which the less common tactical device of trapping is superbly illustrated.

USSR VS. REST OF THE WORLD

White: GM Alexander Beliavsky,
Black: GM Bent Larsen
USSR vs. Rest of the World Challenge Match, London 1984
Caro-Kann Defense, Classical Variation (**4...Bf5**)

1. e4 c6; 2. d4 d5; 3. Nc3 dxe4; 4. Nxe4 Bf5; 5. Ng3 Bg6; 6. h4 h6; 7. Nf3 Nd7; 8. h5 Bh7; 9. Bd3 Ngf6. An odd move, which is rarely seen nowadays—the standard continuation is 9...Bxd3; 10. Qxd3 Qc7; 11. Bd2 e6, with both sides aiming at early queenside castling. **10. Bxh7 Nxh7; 11. Qe2 e6; 12. Bd2 Be7; 13. 0-0-0 Qb6; 14. Ne5 Rd8; 15. Rhe1 0-0?!** Black had to castle sometime, but now White has a cool shot that gains the initiative and eliminates an important Black defender.

16. Ng6! If 16...fxg6, then 17. Qxe6+ will regain the piece with a large advantage. **16...Rfe8; 17. Nxe7+ Rxe7; 18. Nf5! Ree8; 19. Nd6 Rf8; 20. Bf4 Ndf6; 21. Be5 Rd7; 22. Rd3!** A powerful "rook-lift", with the rook eyeing both the king and the queen! **22...Qa5 23. Rg3!** Wait a minute! Can't Black take the a2 pawn? Why don't you look at the next diagram and decide?

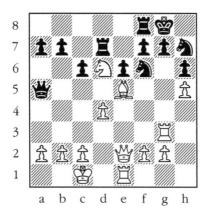

23...Qxa2? loses to 24. Ra3 Qd5; 25. c4! Qxg2; 26. Rg3 Qh2; 27 Rxg7+!, winning Black's queen. This entire sequence is really a very neat trapping combination. But while Larsen doesn't fall for 23...Qxa2?, his next move is also a serious blunder. **23...Rfd8?** This cuts off an essential retreat square for Black's queen. Can you trap her? Take a long, hard look at the following diagram.

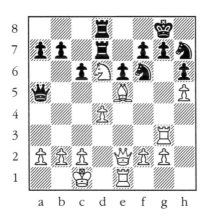

24. Ra3 Qb6; 25. Nc4 Qb4; 26. Bd6!! (A truly elegant trapping combination, as her majesty's escape route is blocked by force.) **Rxd6; 27. c3 Qb5; 28. Ra5 Rd5; 29. Rxb5 cxb5; 30. Ne3 Rxh5; 31. g4! Rh2** (31...Rg5 32. f4!); **32. Qxb5 b6?**

He had to play 32...Rxf2, although after 33. Qxb7, White should win without much difficulty. Now Larsen falls into another trap! **33. Qe5! Rxf2?** (33...Rh3 lasts a little longer); **34. Qg3 Ne4.** Forced, or else the wandering Rook is trapped, but after **35. Qc7!** (gaining a vital tempo!) **Rf8 36. Nd1!** A final discovery finishes Black off. **Larsen resigns**.

In Chapter 3, our grab bag if you will, we have given you 103 challenging situations that could or really did occur in actual play. Although we still give a hint at the top of each diagram, we will not tell you whether you are looking for checkmate, material gain, or merely survival. While we have included many standard tactical themes in this chapter, we are also introducing a few new ones, some of which—such as promotion, unpin, or get out of check—are self-explanatory. However, Bruce has introduced a new tactical term, *Zwischenschach*, which is somewhat akin to the well-known chess tactic *Zwischenzug* (meaning literally an "in-between move"), and has given us several cool examples. *Zwischenschach* simply means playing a surprising and unexpected check that your opponent did not consider when calculating a given sequence of moves.

Capablanca had a unique grasp of the tactical possibilities inherent in any chess position, and in a game from a simultaneous exhibition, he had a very clever idea. Black had literally been copying all of Capa's moves from the first move on, so how did Capa put an end to this?

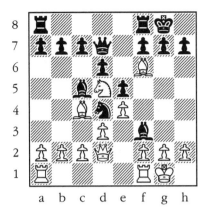

1. Ne7+! (You can't copy a check!) **Kh8; 2. Bxg7+! Kxg7; 3. Qg5+ Kh8; 4. Qf6#.** Incidentally, Black probably expected either 2. Qg5? Rg8 or 2. Qh6 Qg4 with an advantage.

Survival is a somewhat neglected tactical concept although players often have to seek salvation in a draw. Besides mutual agreement, the most common ways to achieve this are by forcing a stalemate, book draw, or perpetual check, and you will find some cute, tricky examples of these in Chapter 3. Recently, Fred needed to find a way to save his butt in the following position against Sarkis Aagian, a very promising junior, during a recent Tuesday Night Masters Tournament at New York City's famous Marshall Chess Club. What did he play?

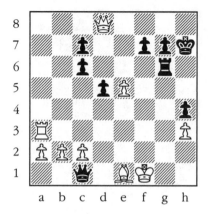

This was a game-in-thirty-minutes (each) tournament, and at this point, Fred had only five minutes left. He thought hard for about 3 1/2 minutes but found no convincing continuation. Remembering he was a piece down, he bailed out with **1... Rg1+!; 2. Kxg1 Qxe1+ draw**. Black has a perpetual check. Sometimes, discretion really is the better part of valor!

Study and practice: it's the only way to get better. We hope that our book will help you knock out whatever competition you face.

Start practicing!

Fred Wilson & Bruce Alberston

CHAPTER 1

CHECKMATE

In the hurly-burly of play it's easy to lose track of what is truly important. This chapter will serve as a reminder that the most valuable piece on the board is the king. Get him and the game is over. First, attack the king, making sure that the checking piece cannot be captured or blocked out. Second, control all the escape squares. Do that, and you've fulfilled the conditions for checkmate.

A king that has lost its pawn cover or is roaming about on an open board is always susceptible to a snap mate-in-one. More commonly, mate has to be set up and often in such a way as not to allow the enemy king to catch his breath and gather his forces for defense. The attacker accomplishes this task with forcing moves, checks, captures, and mate-in-one threats, thereby leading the play down a narrow path that ends in mate.

The positions in this chapter have been taken from actual games, real over-the-board situations that are likely to arise in your own practice. There are no mindbenders or composed problems which some find pernicious to the little gray cells. In short, everything is within reach, though at times you may have to stretch a little as the positions become steadily harder toward the end.

1.
White to Move
(Mating Net)

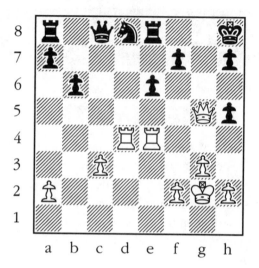

2.
Black to Move
(Mating Net)

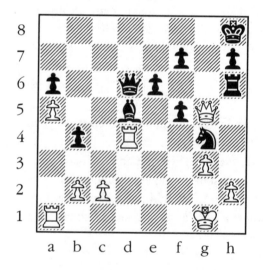

3.
Black to Move
(Mating Net)

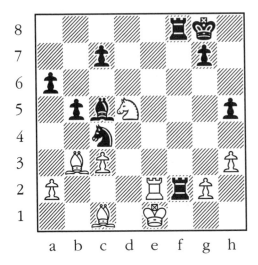

4.
White to Move
(Mating Net)

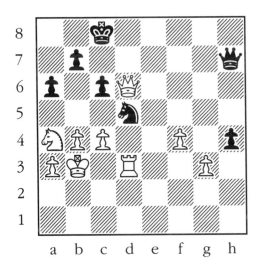

5.
Black to Move
(Mating Net)

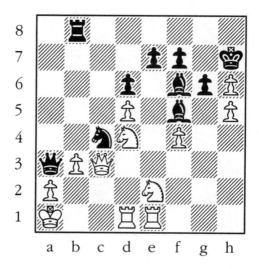

6.
White to Move
(Mating Net)

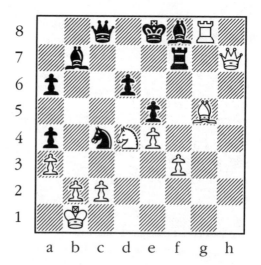

7.
Black to Move
(Mating Net)

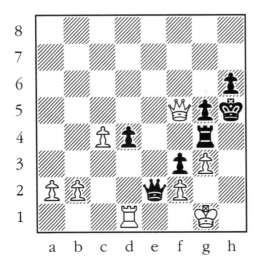

8.
Black to Move
(Mating Net)

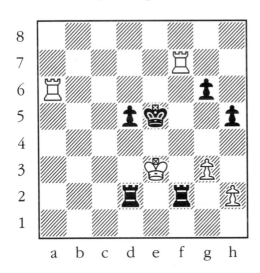

9.
White to Move
(Mating Net)

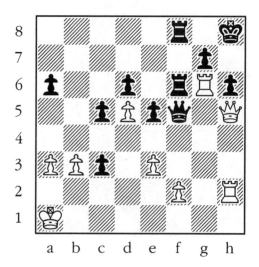

10.
White to Move
(Mating Net)

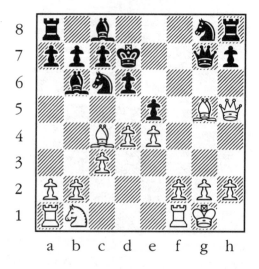

11.
Black to Move
(Mating Net)

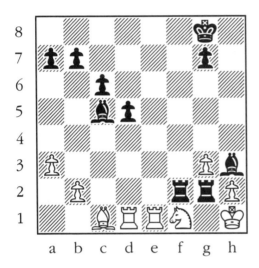

12.
Black to Move
(Mating Net)

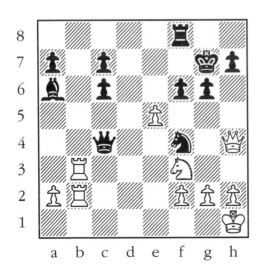

13.
White to Move
(Mating Net)

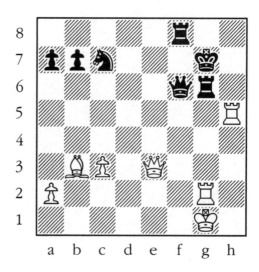

14.
White to Move
(Mating Net)

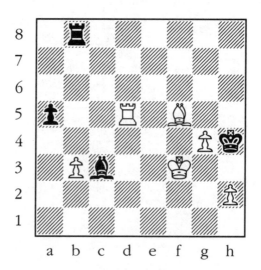

15.
Black to Move
(Mating Net)

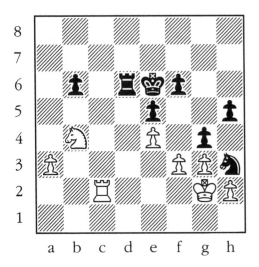

16.
White to Move
(Mating Net)

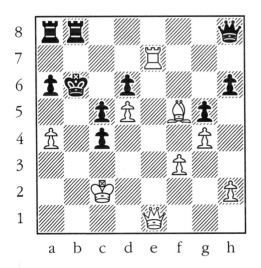

17.
White to Move
(Mating Net)

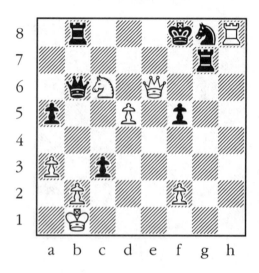

18.
White to Move
(Mating Net)

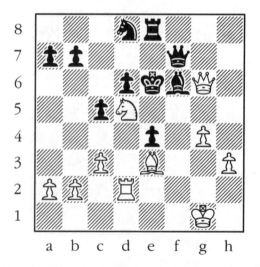

19.
Black to Move
(Mating Net)

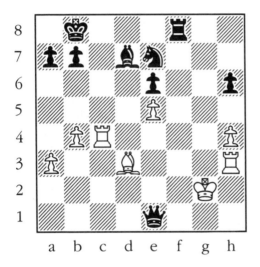

20.
White to Move
(Mating Net)

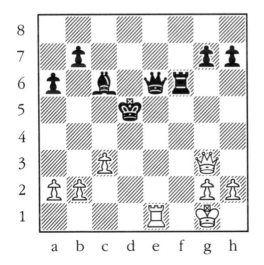

21.
White to Move
(Mating Net)

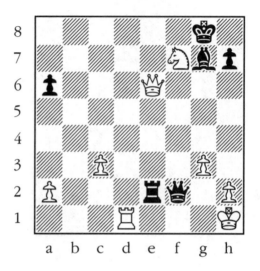

22.
White to Move
(Mating Net)

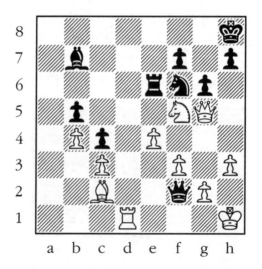

23.
White to Move
(Mating Net)

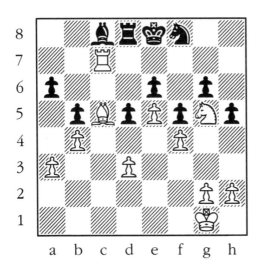

24.
Black to Move
(Mating Net)

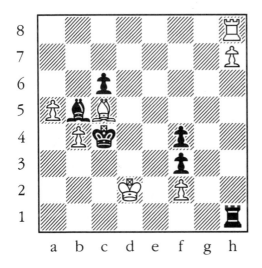

25.
Black to Play
(Mating Attack)

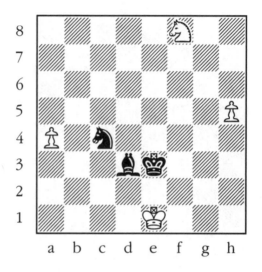

26.
White to Play
(Mating Attack)

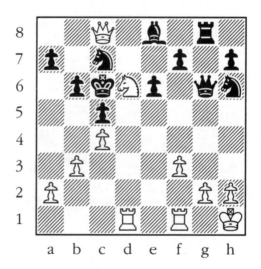

27.
White to Play
(Mating Attack)

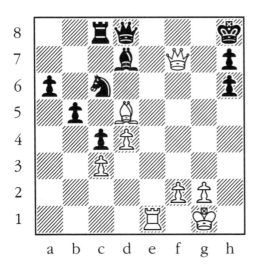

28.
White to Play
(Mating Attack)

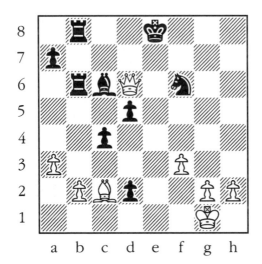

29.
White to Play
(Mating Attack)

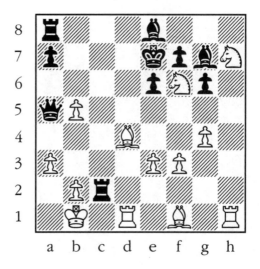

30.
White to Play
(Mating Attack)

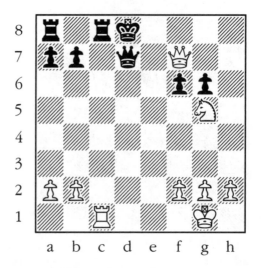

31.
Black to Play
(Mating Attack)

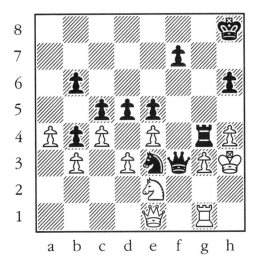

32.
White to Play
(Mating Attack)

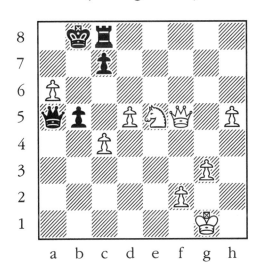

33.
Black to Play
(Mating Attack)

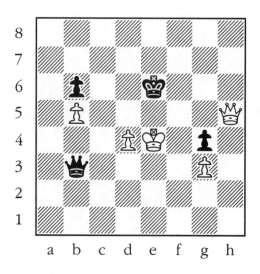

34.
Black to Play
(Mating Attack)

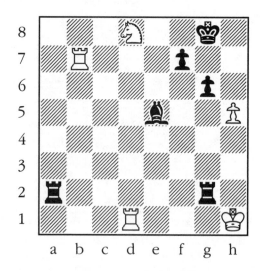

35.
Black to Move
(Mating Net)

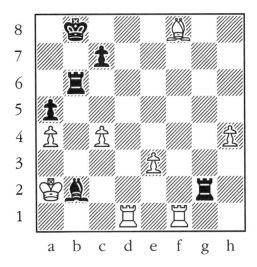

36.
Black to Move
(Mating Net)

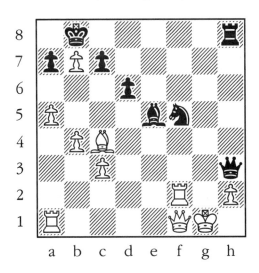

37.
White to Move
(Mating Net)

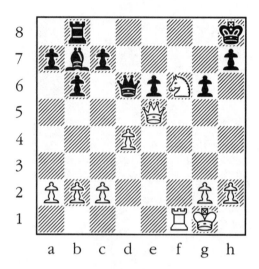

38.
White to Move
(Mating Net)

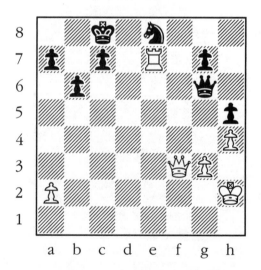

39.
White to Move
(Mating Net)

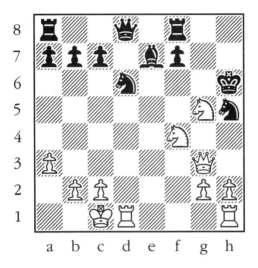

40.
Black to Move
(Mating Net)

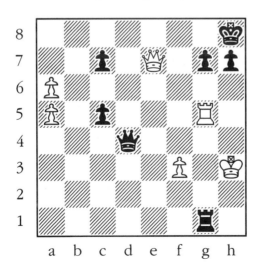

41.
White to Move
(Mating Net)

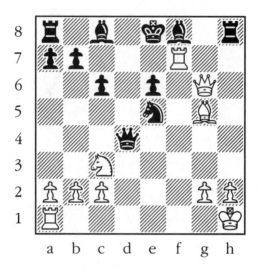

42.
White to Move
(Mating Net)

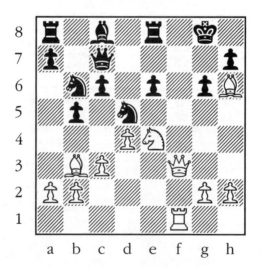

43.
Black to Move
(Mating Net)

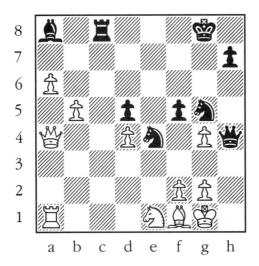

44.
White to Move
(Mating Net)

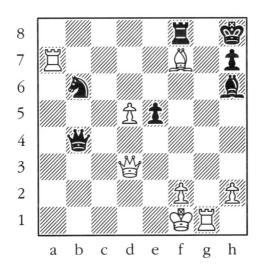

45.
White to Move
(Mating Net)

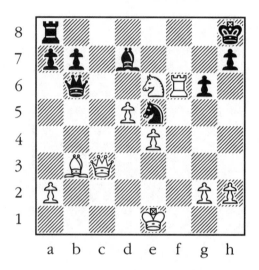

46.
White to Move
(Mating Net)

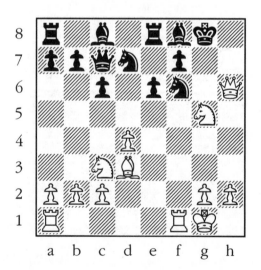

47.
White to Move
(Mating Net)

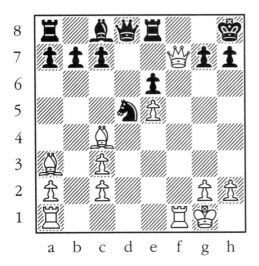

48.
White to Move
(Mating Net)

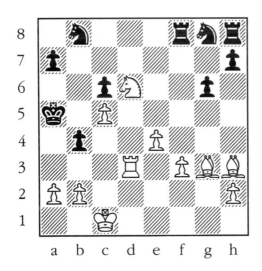

49.
Black to Move
(Mating Net)

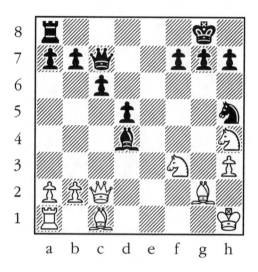

50.
White to Move
(Mating Net)

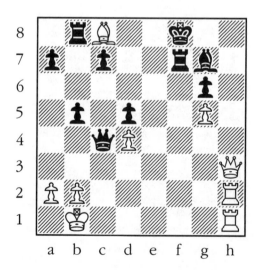

51.
White to Move
(Mating Net)

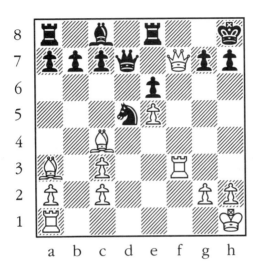

52.
White to Move
(Mating Net)

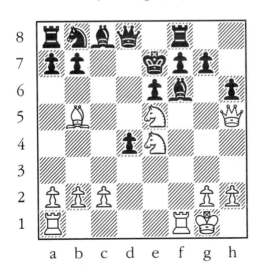

53.
White to Move
(Mating Net)

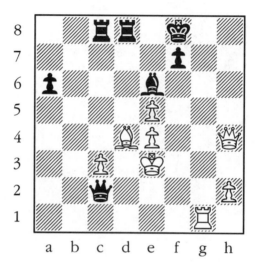

54.
Black to Move
(Mating Net)

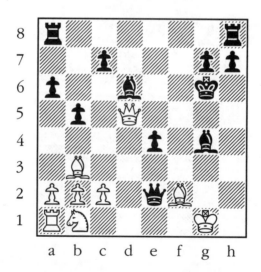

55.
White to Move
(Mating Net)

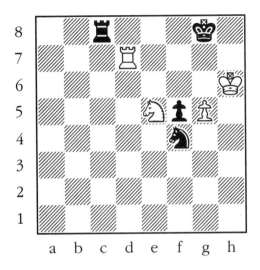

56.
White to Move
(Mating Net)

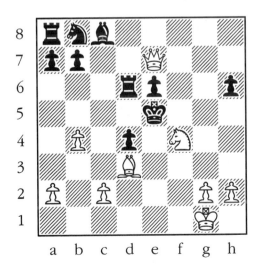

57.
White to Move
(Mating Net)

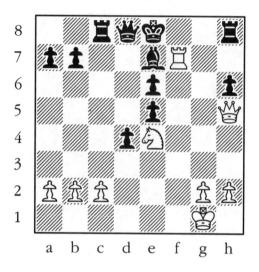

58.
Black to Move
(Mating Net)

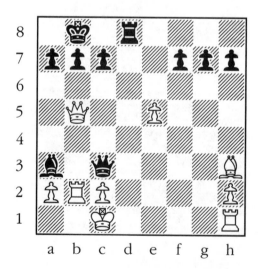

59.
Black to Move
(Mating Net)

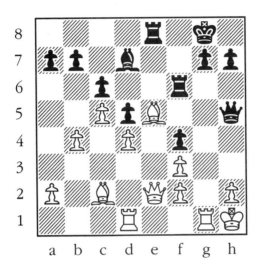

60.
Black to Move
(Mating Net)

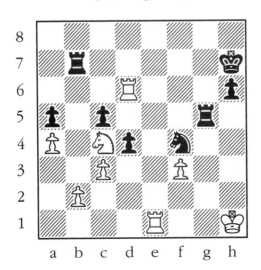

61.
White to Move
(Mating Net)

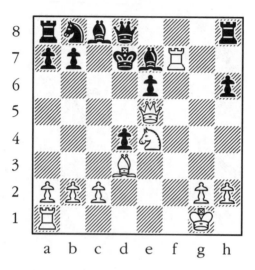

62.
White to Move
(Mating Net)

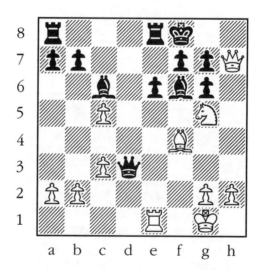

63.
White to Move
(Mating Net)

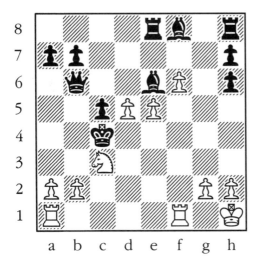

64.
White to Move
(Mating Net)

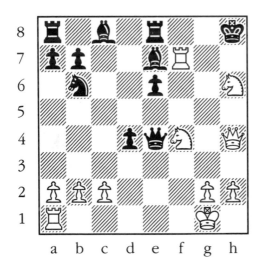

65.
Black to Move
(Mating Net)

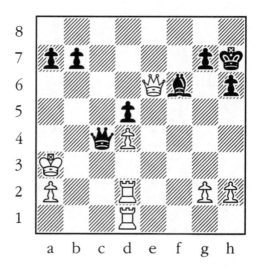

66.
Black to Move
(Mating Net)

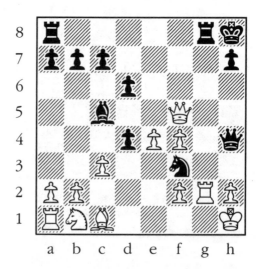

67.
Black to Move
(Mating Net)

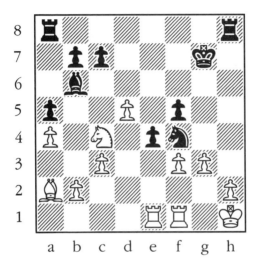

68.
White to Move
(Mating Net)

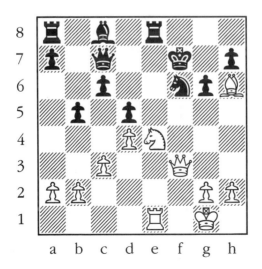

69.
White to Move
(Mating Net)

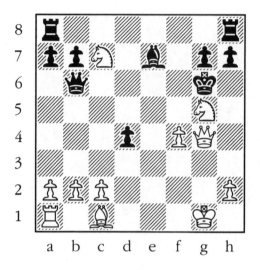

70.
White to Move
(Mating Net)

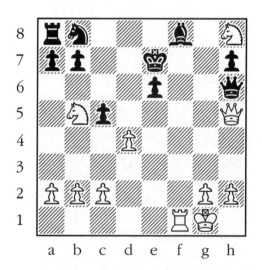

71.
Black to Move
(Mating Net)

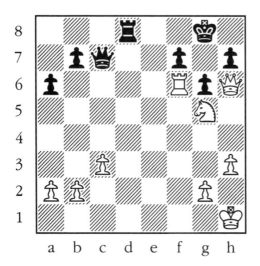

72.
White to Move
(Mating Net)

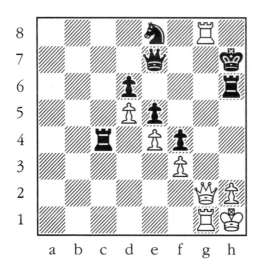

73.
White to Move
(Mating Net)

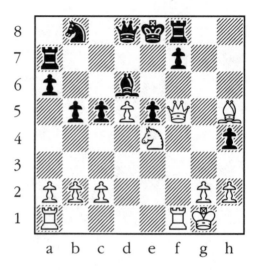

74.
White to Move
(Mating Net)

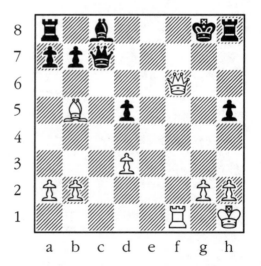

75.
White to Move
(Mating Net)

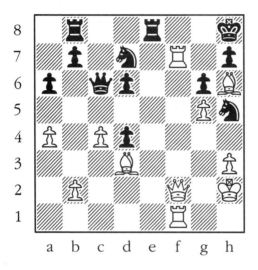

76.
White to Move
(Mating Net)

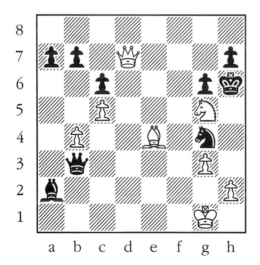

77.
Black to Move
(Mating Net)

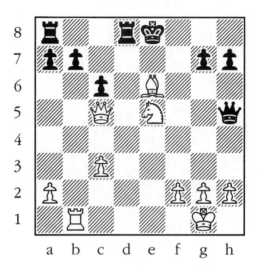

78.
White to Move
(Mating Net)

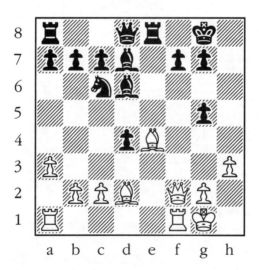

79.
White to Move
(Mating Net)

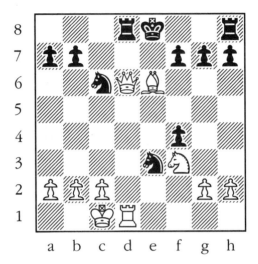

80.
White to Move
(Mating Net)

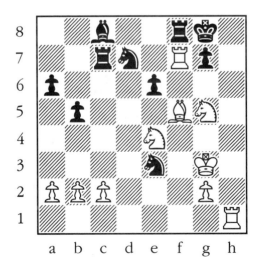

81.
White to Move
(Mating Net)

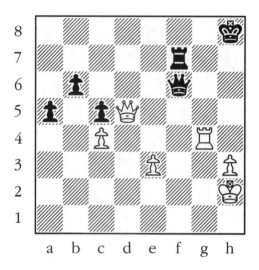

82.
White to Move
(Mating Net)

83.
White to Move
(Mating Net)

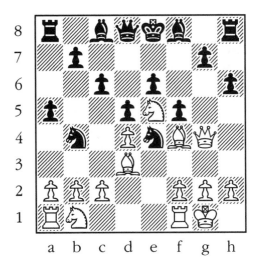

84.
White to Move
(Mating Net)

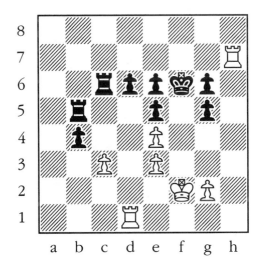

85.
White to Move
(Mating Net)

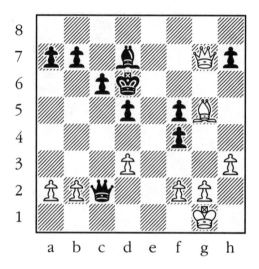

86.
Black to Move
(Mating Net)

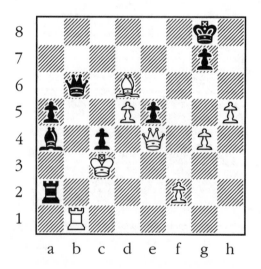

87.
White to Move
(Mating Net)

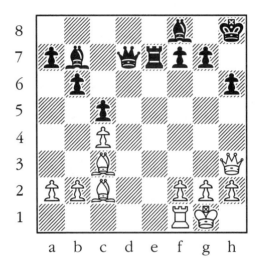

88.
White to Move
(Mating Net)

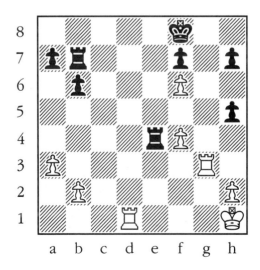

89.
White to Move
(Mating Net)

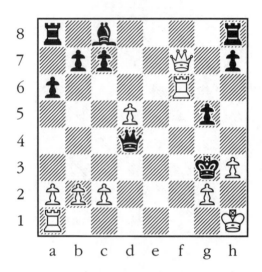

90.
White to Move
(Mating Net)

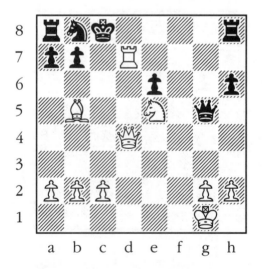

91.
White to Move
(Mating Net)

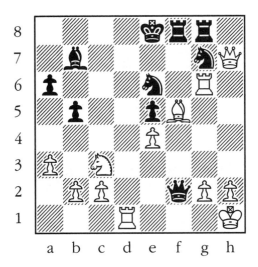

92.
White to Move
(Mating Net)

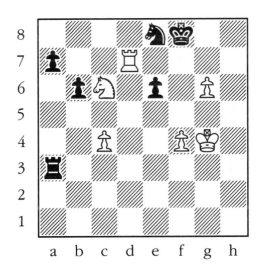

93.
White to Move
(Mating Net)

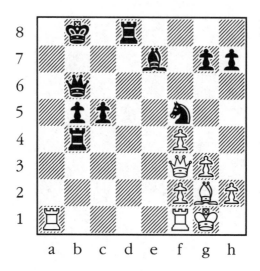

94.
Black to Move
(Mating Net)

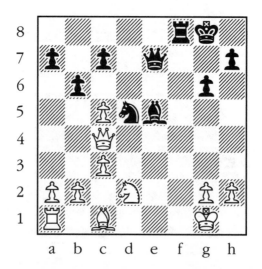

95.
Black to Move
(Mating Net)

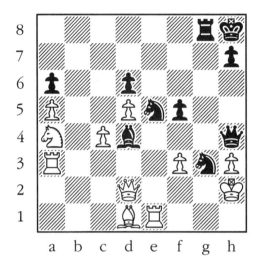

96.
White to Move
(Mating Net)

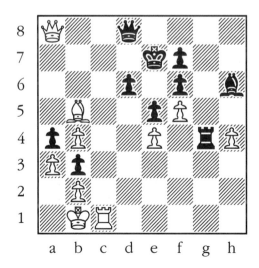

97.
Black to Move
(Mating Net)

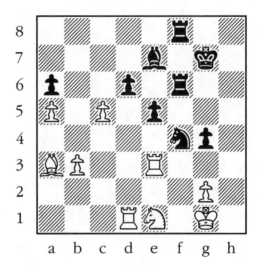

98.
Black to Move
(Mating Net)

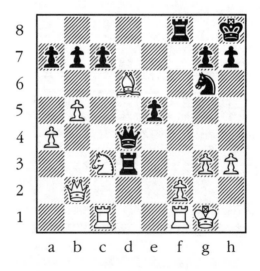

99.
White to Move
(Mating Net)

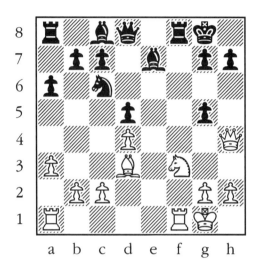

100.
White to Move
(Mating Net)

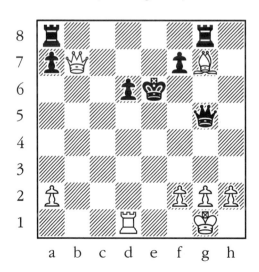

CHAPTER 2

WINNING MATERIAL

The basic fact of life on the chessboard is that the larger army wins. So in the following chapter we mainly concern ourselves with looking for ways to gain a material advantage. Here we examine the ten most common ways to win the opponent's pieces. In the mating attack, the defender is able to ward off the threats to his king only by parting with material. Double attacks, where two of the enemy pieces are under fire, are illustrated by forks, pins, skewers, and discoveries. Surrounding and then capturing a piece comes under the heading of trapping. Undermining the defense is yet another way to gain an advantage. Typical ploys are removing the guard, driving off, and overloading. Finally, a player can add to his arsenal by promoting pawns into queens.

101.
White to Move
(Mating Attack)

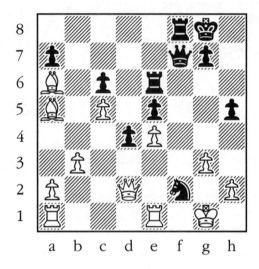

102.
Black to Move
(Mating Attack)

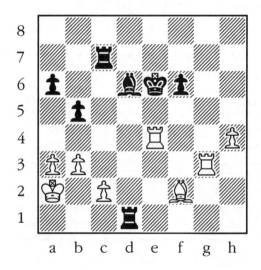

103.
White to Move
(Mating Attack)

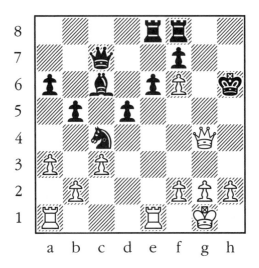

104.
Black to Move
(Mating Attack)

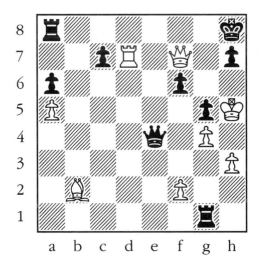

105.
White to Move
(Mating Attack)

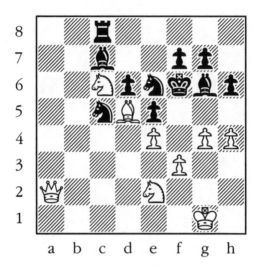

106.
Black to Move
(Fork)

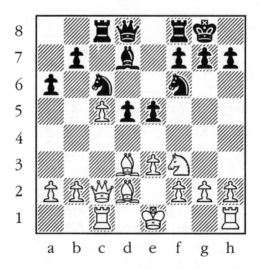

107.
White to Move
(Fork)

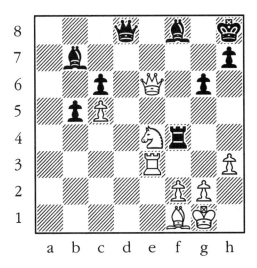

108.
White to Move
(Fork)

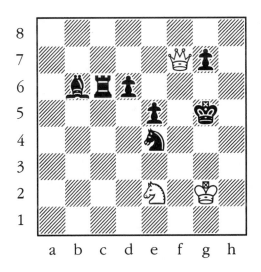

109.
White to Move
(Fork)

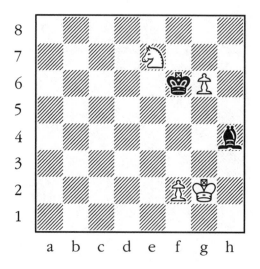

110.
Black to Move
(Fork)

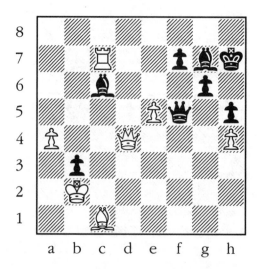

111.
Black to Move
(Pin)

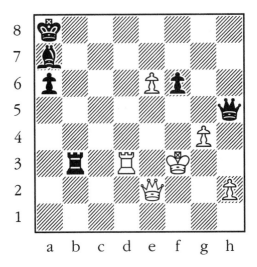

112.
White to Move
(Pin)

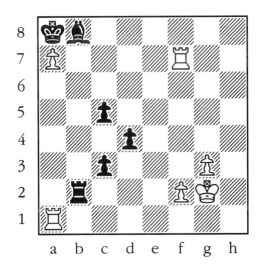

113.
Black to Move
(Pin)

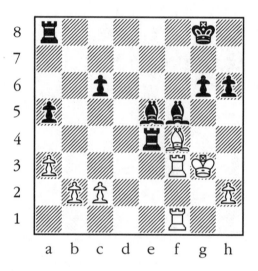

114.
White to Move
(Pin)

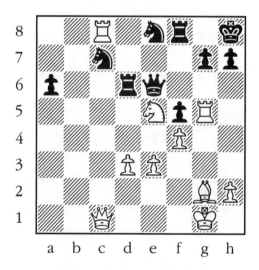

115.
White to Move
(Pin)

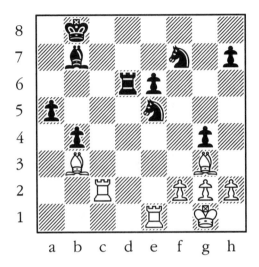

116.
Black to Move
(Skewer)

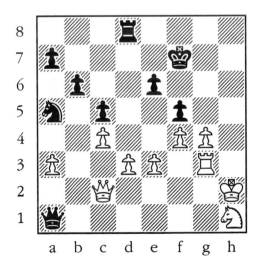

117.
White to Move
(Skewer)

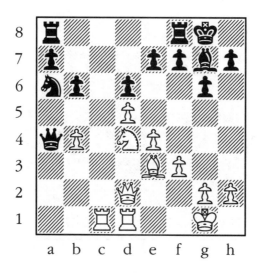

118.
Black to Move
(Skewer)

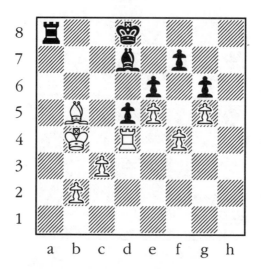

119.
White to Move
(Skewer)

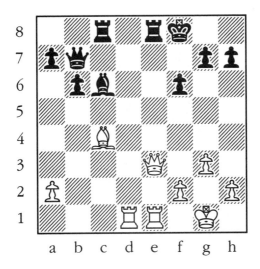

120.
Black to Move
(Skewer)

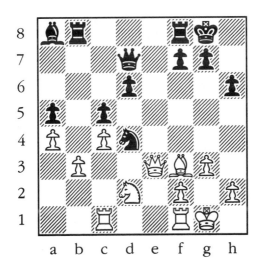

121.
White to Move
(Discovery)

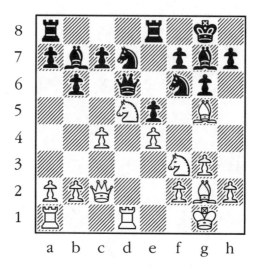

122.
White to Move
(Discovery)

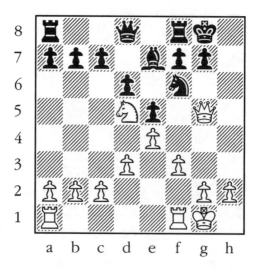

123.
Black to Move
(Discovery)

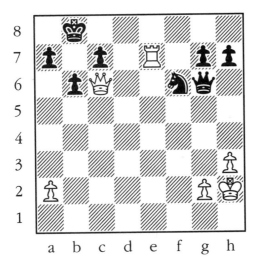

124.
White to Move
(Discovery)

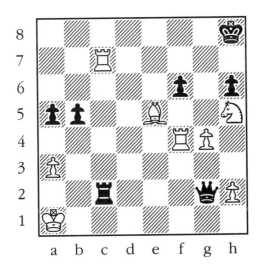

125.
Black to Move
(Discovery)

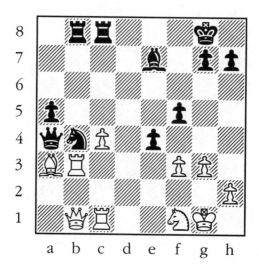

126.
Black to Move
(Trapping)

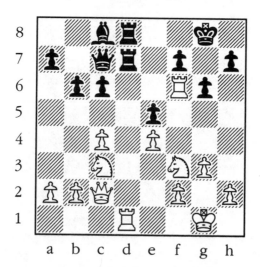

127.
Black to Move
(Trapping)

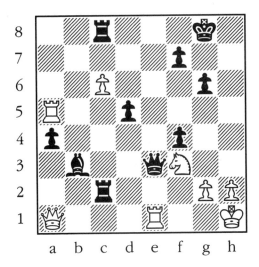

128.
White to Move
(Trapping)

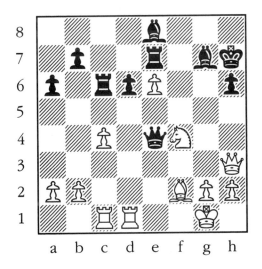

129.
Black to Move
(Trapping)

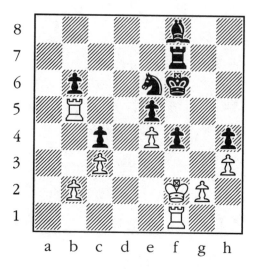

130.
White to Move
(Trapping)

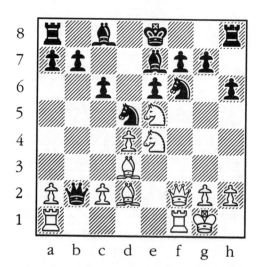

131.
Black to Move
(Removing the Guard)

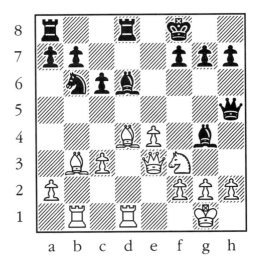

132.
White to Move
(Removing the Guard)

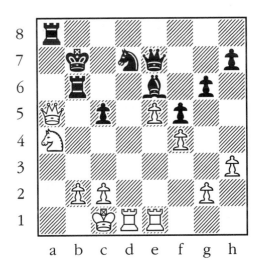

133.
Black to Move
(Removing the Guard)

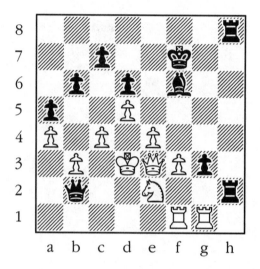

134.
Black to Move
(Removing the Guard)

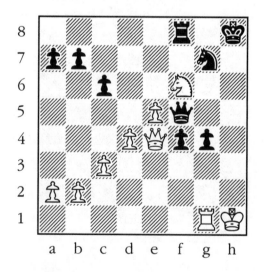

135.
White to Move
(Removing the Guard)

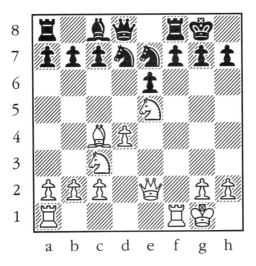

136.
White to Move
(Promotion)

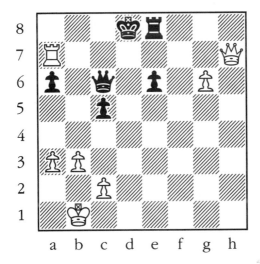

137.
Black to Move
(Promotion)

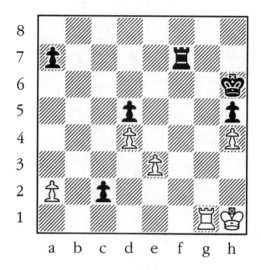

138.
Black to Move
(Promotion)

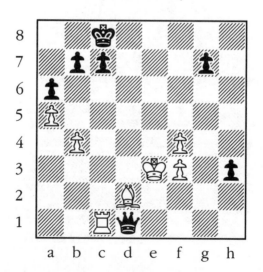

139.
Black to Move
(Promotion)

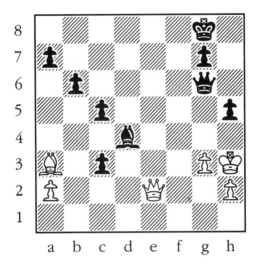

140.
White to Move
(Promotion)

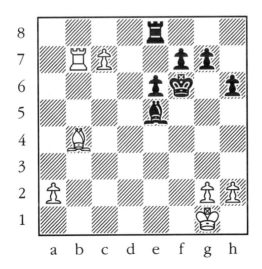

141.
Black to Move
(Driving Off)

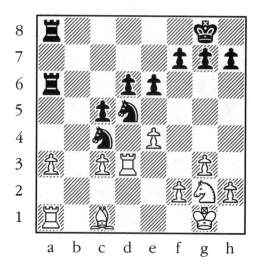

142.
White to Move
(Driving Off)

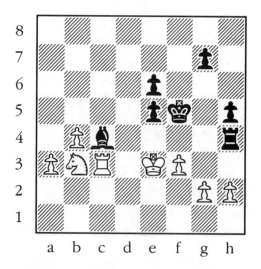

143.
Black to Move
(Driving Off)

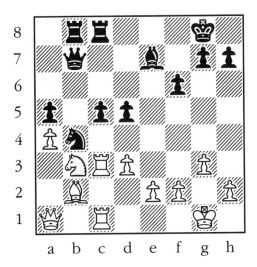

144.
White to Move
(Driving Off)

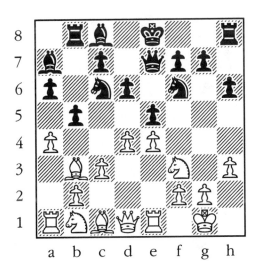

145.
Black to Move
(Driving Off)

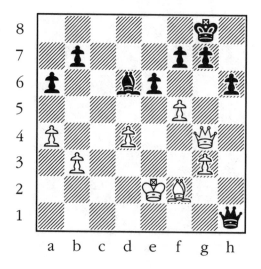

146.
White to Move
(Overload)

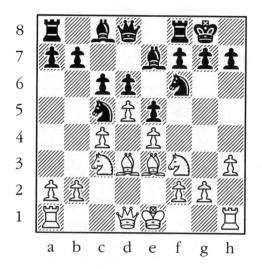

147.
Black to Move
(Overload)

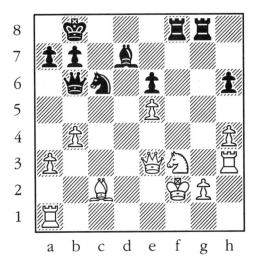

148.
Black to Move
(Overload)

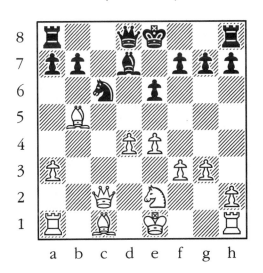

149.
White to Move
(Overload)

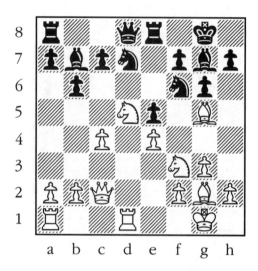

150.
White to Move
(Overload)

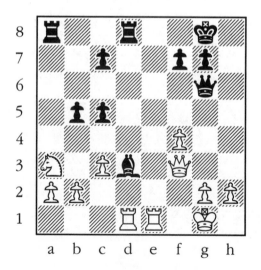

151.
White to Move
(Mating Attack)

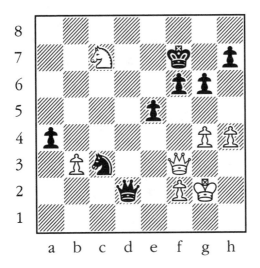

152.
Black to Move
(Mating Attack)

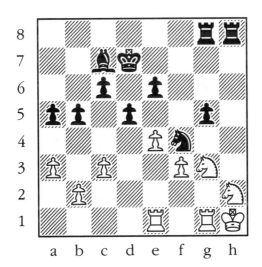

153.
White to Move
(Mating Attack)

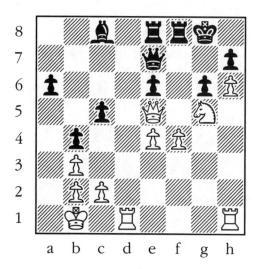

154.
Black to Move
(Mating Attack)

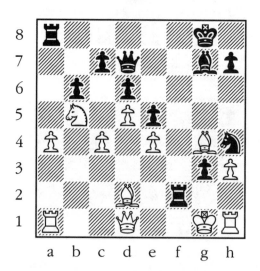

155.
White to Move
(Mating Attack)

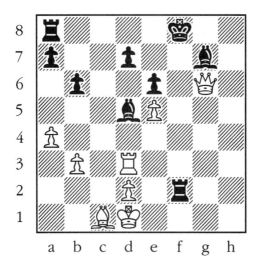

156.
Black to Move
(Fork)

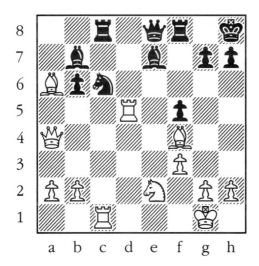

157.
White to Move
(Fork)

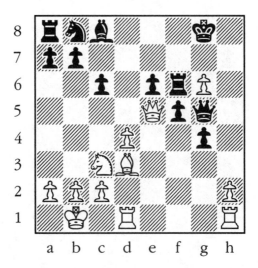

158.
White to Move
(Fork)

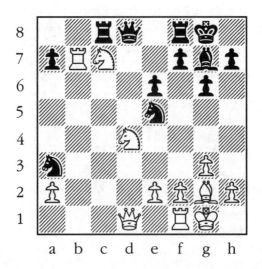

159.
White to Move
(Fork)

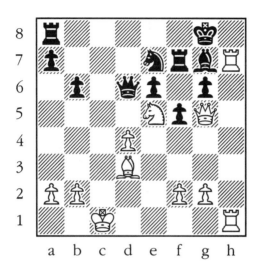

160.
Black to Move
(Fork)

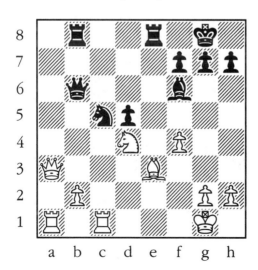

161.
Black to Move
(Pin)

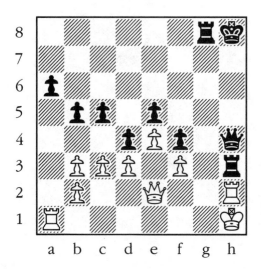

162.
White to Move
(Pin)

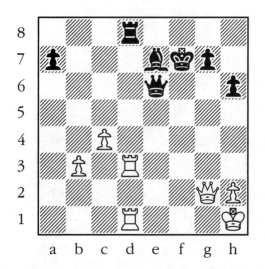

163.
Black to Move
(Pin)

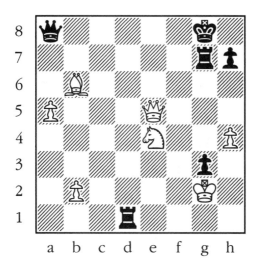

164.
Black to Move
(Pin)

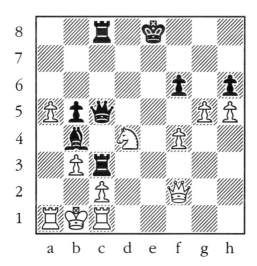

165.
White to Move
(Pin)

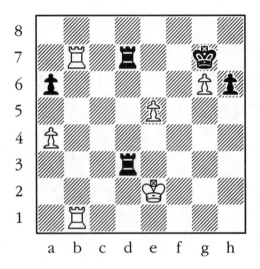

166.
White to Move
(Skewer)

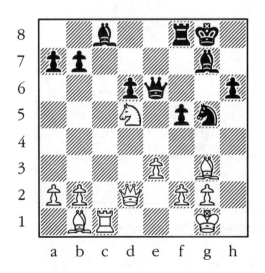

167.
Black to Move
(Skewer)

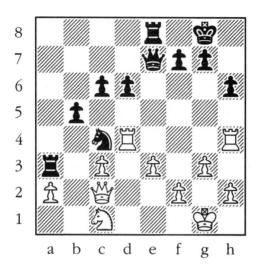

168.
White to Move
(Skewer)

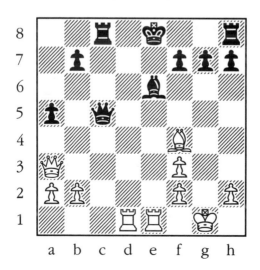

169.
Black to Move
(Skewer)

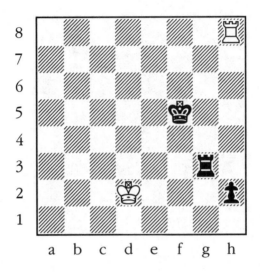

170.
White to Move
(Skewer)

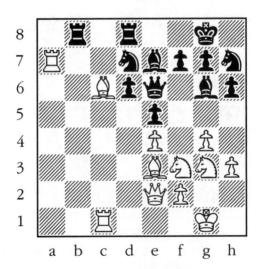

171.
Black to Move
(Discovery)

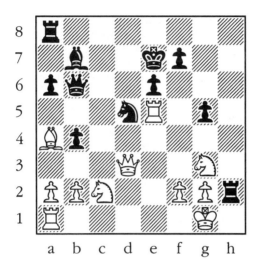

172.
White to Move
(Discovery)

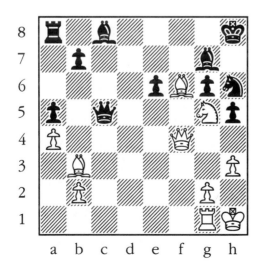

173.
Black to Move
(Discovery)

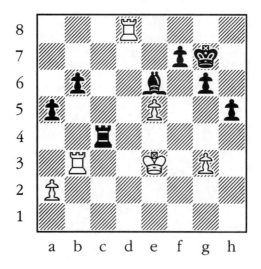

174.
Black to Move
(Discovery)

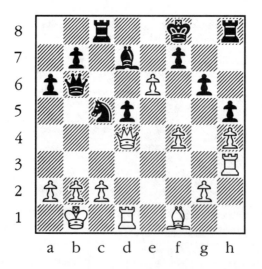

175.
Black to Move
(Discovery)

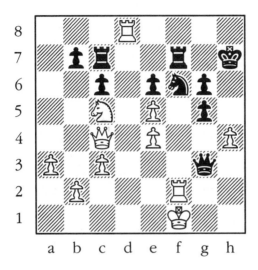

176.
Black to Move
(Trapping)

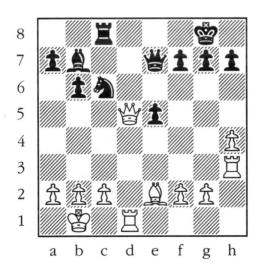

177.
Black to Move
(Trapping)

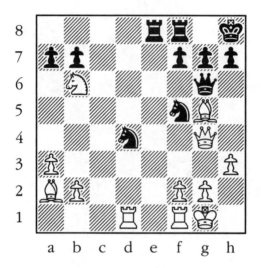

178.
Black to Move
(Trapping)

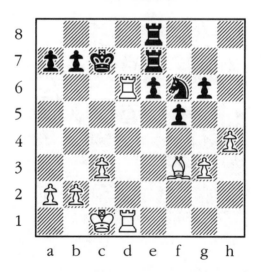

179.
Black to Move
(Trapping)

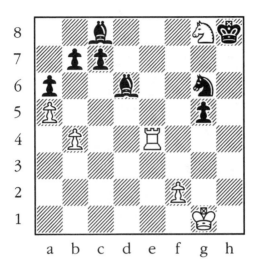

180.
Black to Move
(Trapping)

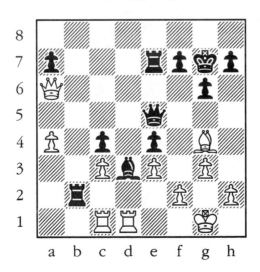

109

181.
Black to Move
(Removing the Guard)

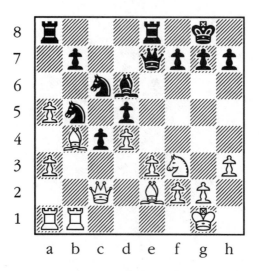

182.
White to Move
(Removing the Guard)

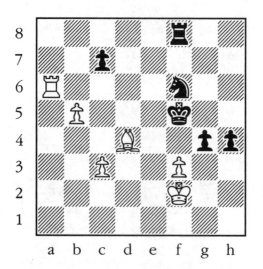

183.
Black to Move
(Removing the Guard)

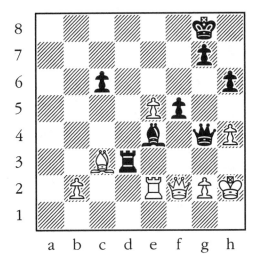

184.
White to Move
(Removing the Guard)

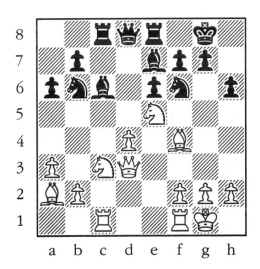

185.
White to Move
(Removing the Guard)

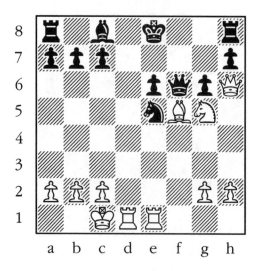

186.
Black to Move
(Promotion)

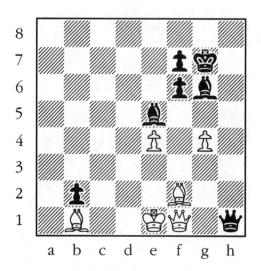

187.
Black to Move
(Promotion)

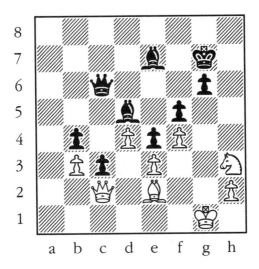

188.
Black to Move
(Promotion)

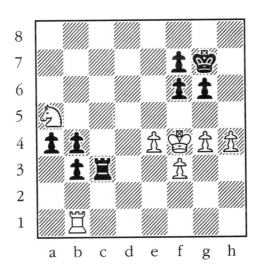

189.
White to Move
(Promotion)

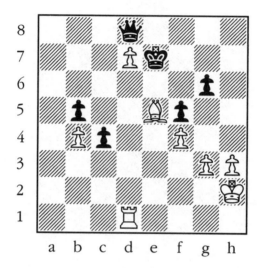

190.
White to Move
(Promotion)

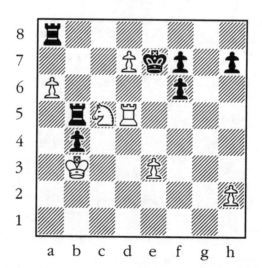

191.
Black to Move
(Driving Off)

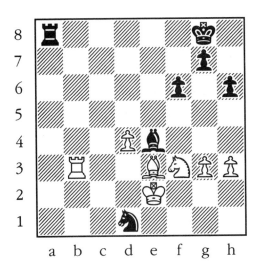

192.
Black to Move
(Driving Off)

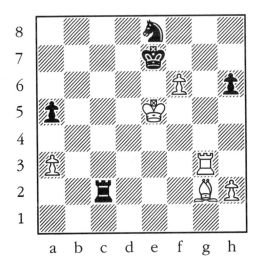

193.
Black to Move
(Driving Off)

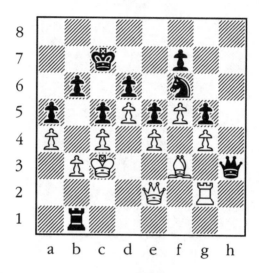

194.
White to Move
(Driving Off)

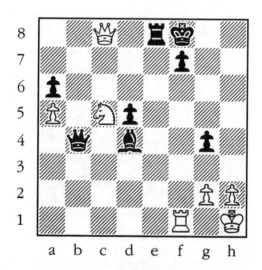

195.
White to Move
(Driving Off)

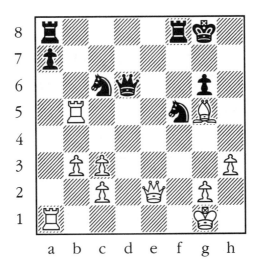

196.
White to Move
(Overload)

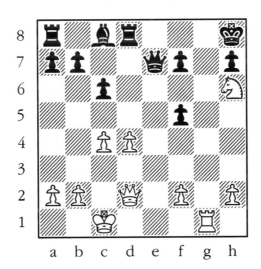

197.
Black to Move
(Overload)

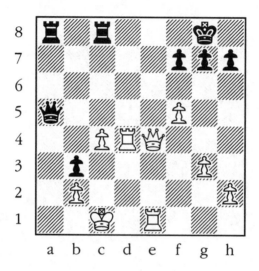

198.
Black to Move
(Overload)

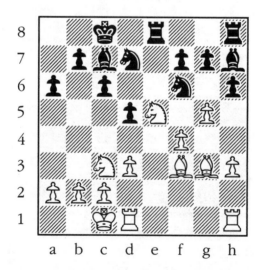

199.
White to Move
(Overload)

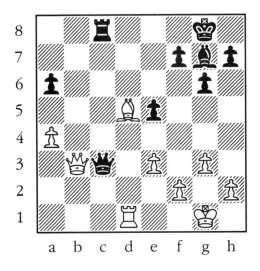

200.
Black to Move
(Overload)

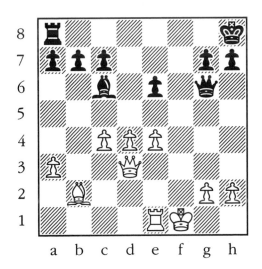

CHAPTER 3

MIXED BAG

In the first two chapters we told you in advance what to look for—mate or win material. Naturally, many of the same themes reappear in this chapter, but now you have to figure out what to play for on your own.

In addition we've added a whole grab bag of themes not encountered in previous chapters. The idea is to simulate real game situations in which there are no advanced clues and you're asked to do whatever the position requires.

For example, don't assume that the side to play is currently winning. In many cases, you're asked to find a defensive move that will ward off the enemy threats and simply maintain the balance.

The final three positions are culled from the realm of endgame studies. In appearance they are game-like, but they are in fact composed positions. So expect to find some artistry, some elegance, and something unexpected. What all three do have in common is that mate figures into the proceedings.

Again, the easier positions come at the beginning of the chapter, the harder ones later on.

201.
Black to Move
(Unpin)

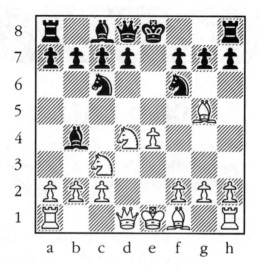

202.
White to Move
(Double Threat)

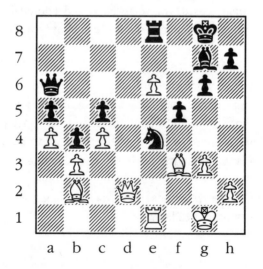

203.
Black to Move
(Get Out of Check)

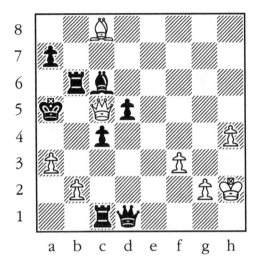

204.
White to Move
(Interference)

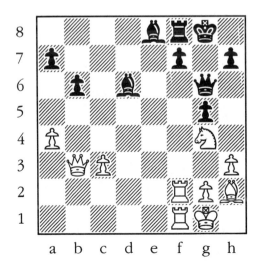

205.
White to Move
(Jettison)

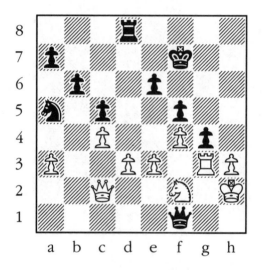

206.
White to Move
(Stalemate)

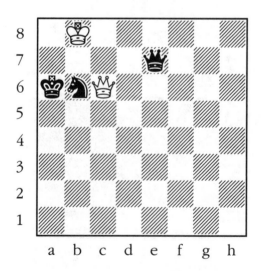

207.
White to Move
(Direct Attack)

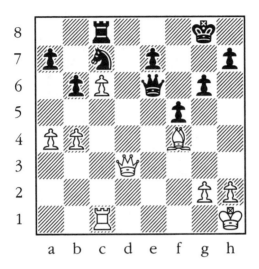

208.
Black to Move
(Zugswang)

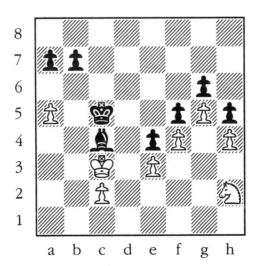

209.
Black to Move
(En Prise)

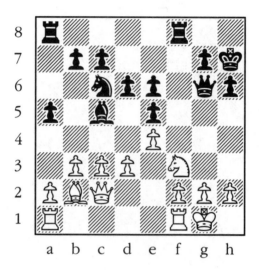

210.
Black to Move
(Fork)

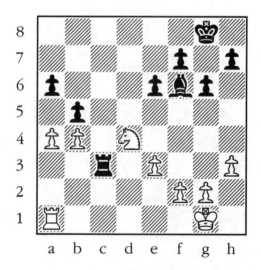

211.
Black to Move
(Defense)

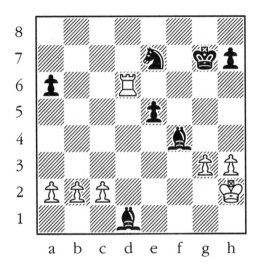

212.
White to Move
(Unpin)

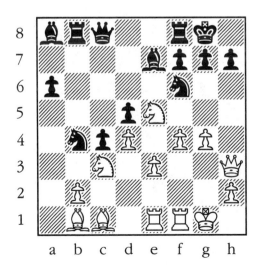

213.
White to Move
(Double Threat)

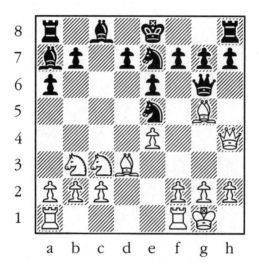

214.
White to Move
(Zwischenschach)

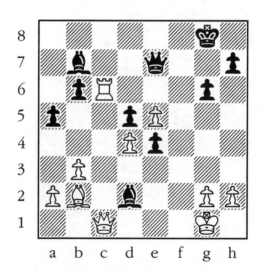

215.
Black to Move
(Fork)

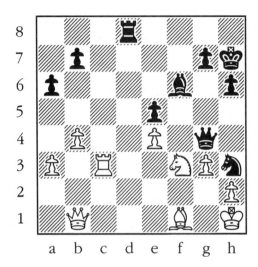

216.
Black to Move
(Defense)

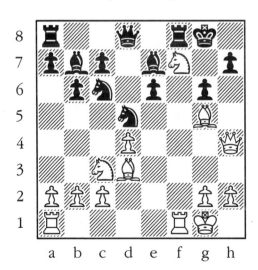

217.
Black to Move
(Interference)

218.
Black to Move
(Jettison)

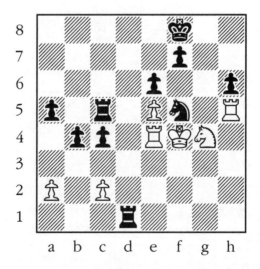

219.
Black to Move
(Saving by Threatening)

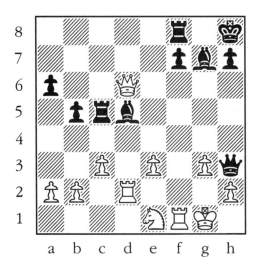

220.
Black to Move
(En Prise)

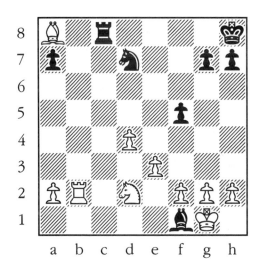

221.
Black to Move
(Defense)

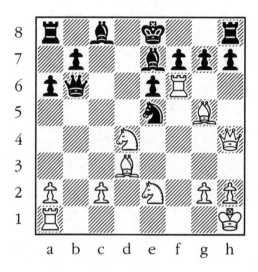

222.
White to Move
(Unpin)

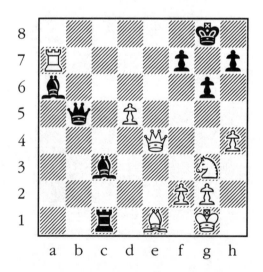

223.
Black to Move
(Double Threat)

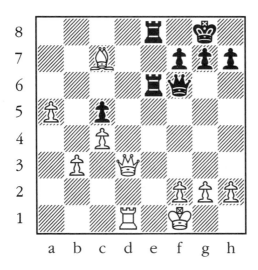

224.
Black to Move
(Deflection)

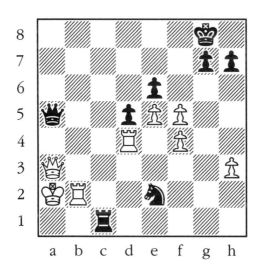

133

225.
White to Move
(Zwischenschach)

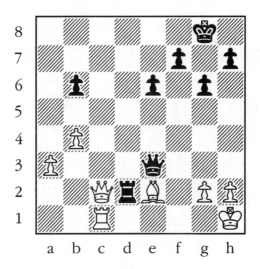

226.
Black to Move
(Defense)

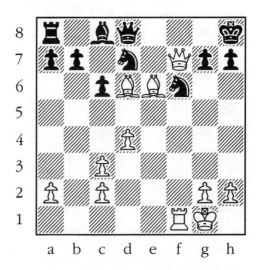

227.
White to Move
(Zwischenzug)

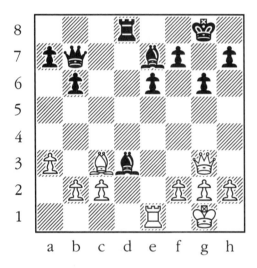

228.
White to Move
(Get Out Of Check)

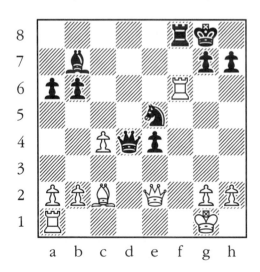

229.
White to Move
(Saving by checking)

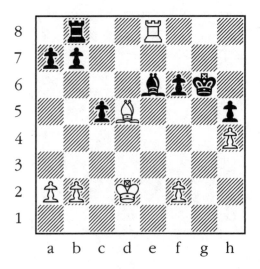

230.
Black to Move
(Fork)

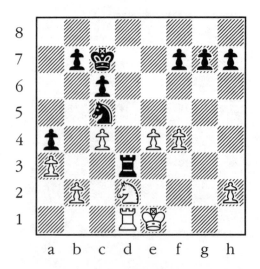

231.
Black to Move
(Defense)

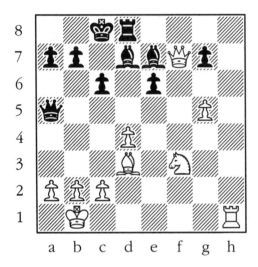

232.
White to Move
(Back Rank)

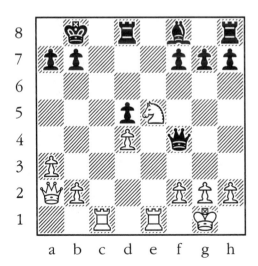

233.
Black to Move
(Double Threat)

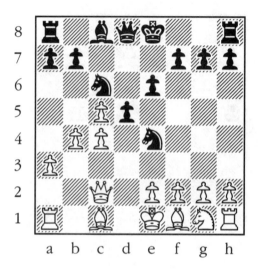

234.
White to Move
(Deflection)

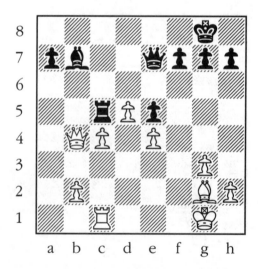

235.
Black to Move
(Zwischenschach)

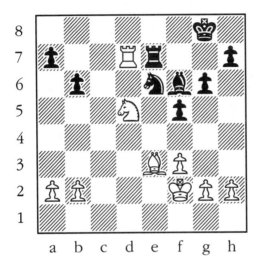

236.
White to Move
(Get Out Of Check)

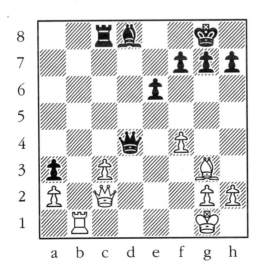

237.
Black to Move
(En Prise)

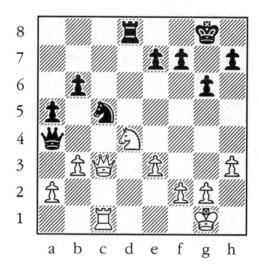

238.
Black to Move
(Pin)

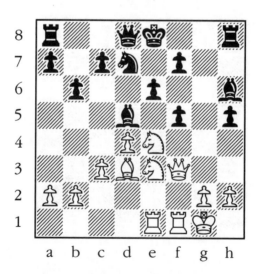

239.
Black to Move
(Removing the Guard)

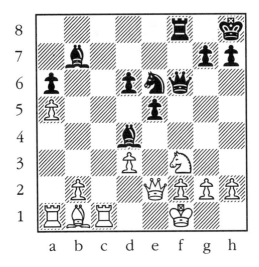

240.
White to Move
(Driving Off)

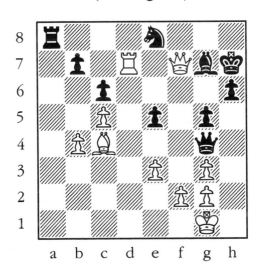

241.
Black to Move
(Defense)

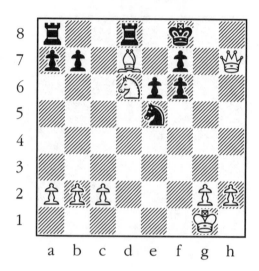

242.
White to Move
(Unpin)

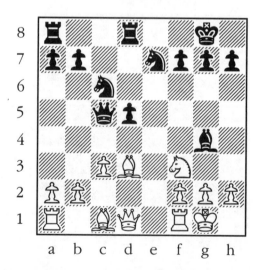

243.
White to Move
(Back Rank)

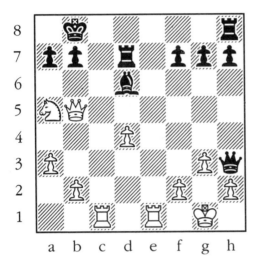

244.
White to Move
(Double Threat)

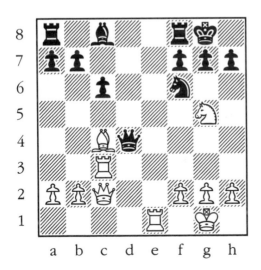

245.
White to Move
(Simplification)

246.
White to Move
(Deflection)

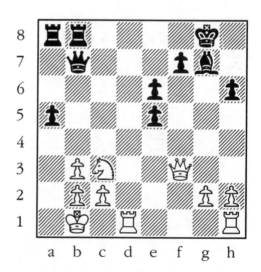

247.
Black to Move
(Zwischenschach)

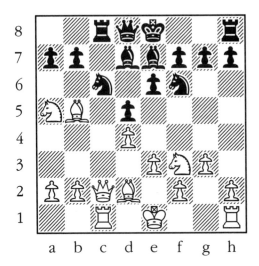

248.
Black to Move
(Get Out of Check)

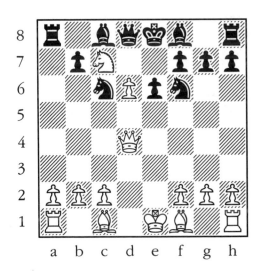

249.
Black to Move
(Book Draw)

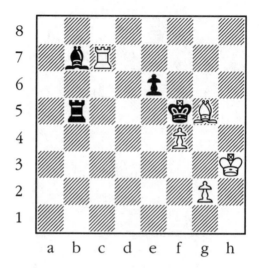

250.
Black to Move
(En Prise)

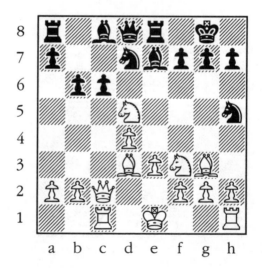

251.
Black to Move
(Defense)

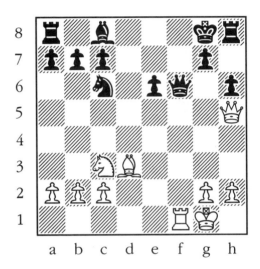

252.
Black to Move
(Unpin)

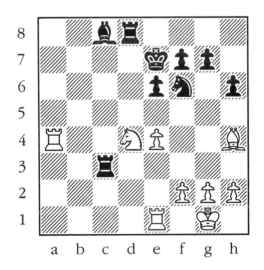

253.
Black to Move
(Back Rank)

254.
Black to Move
(Double Attack)

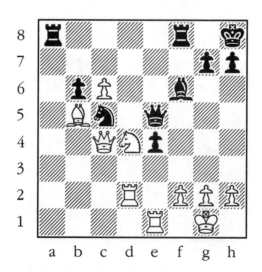

255.
White to Move
(Deflection)

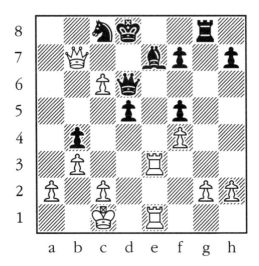

256.
White to Move
(Unpin)

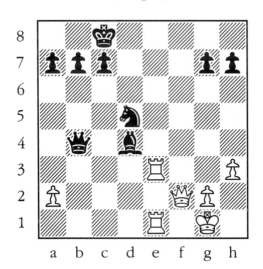

257.
White to Move
(Zwischenschach)

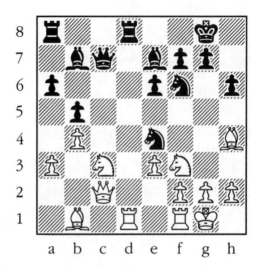

258.
Black to Move
(Get Out of Check)

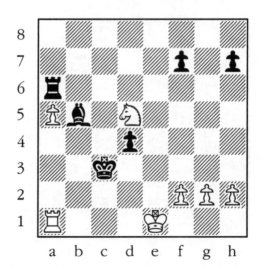

259.
White to Move
(Perpetual Check)

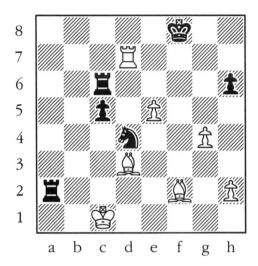

260.
Black to Move
(En Prise)

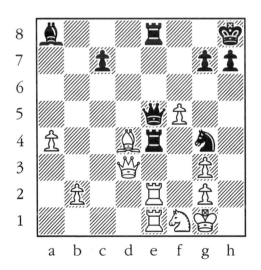

261.
White to Move
(X-Ray)

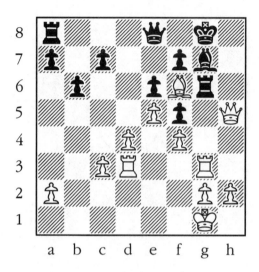

262.
Black to Move
(Unpin)

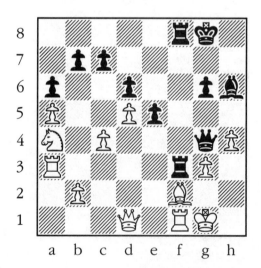

263.
White to Move
(Back Rank)

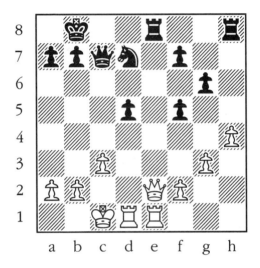

264.
White to Move
(Double Threat)

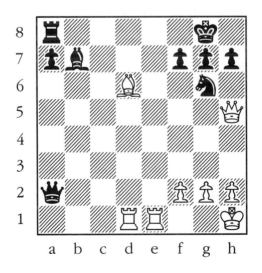

265.
White to Move
(Simplification)

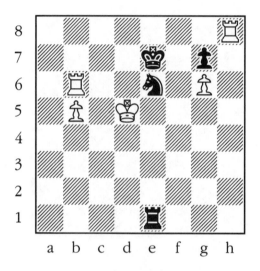

266.
White to Move
(Zwischenschach)

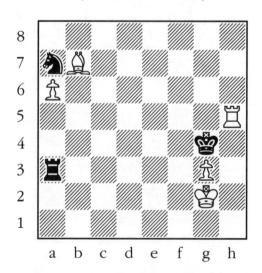

267.
White to Move
(Line Opening)

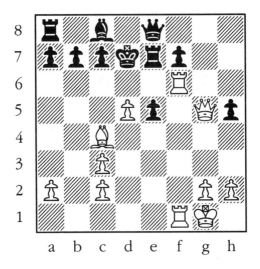

268.
White to Move
(Fortress)

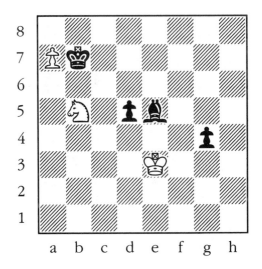

269.
White to Move
(Meeting the Threat)

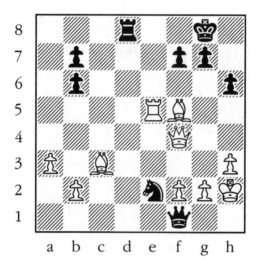

270.
Black to Move
(En Prise)

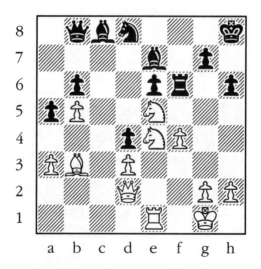

271.
Black to Move
(Defense)

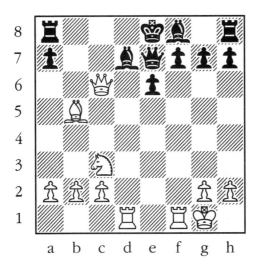

272.
White to Move
(Unpin)

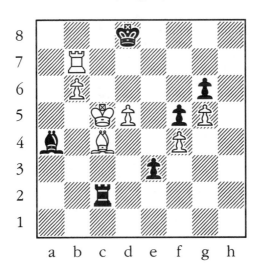

273.
White to Move
(Back Rank)

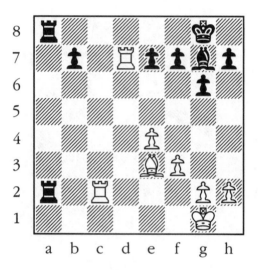

274.
White to Move
(Double Threat)

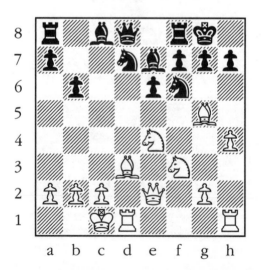

275.
White to Move
(Simplification)

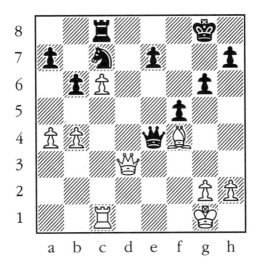

276.
White to Move
(Deflection)

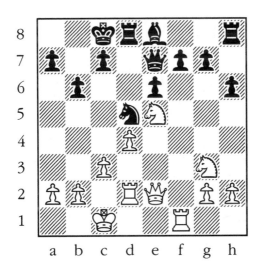

277.
White to Move
(Zwischenschach)

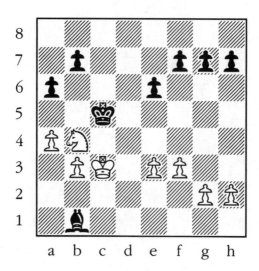

278.
White to Move
(Open Lines)

279.
Black to Move
(Stalemate)

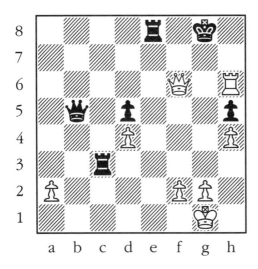

280.
Black to Move
(Mating Attack)

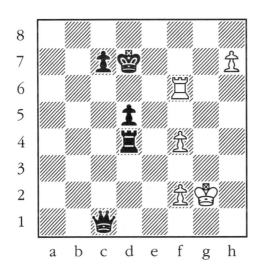

281.
White to Move
(Triangulation)

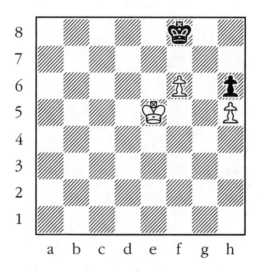

282.
White to Move
(Unpin)

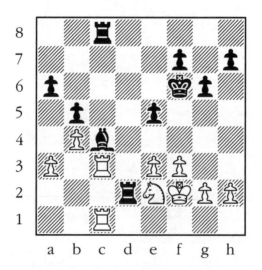

283.
Black to Move
(Back Rank)

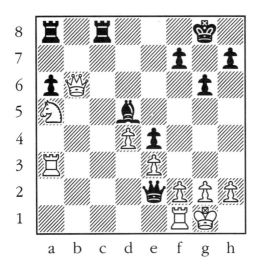

284.
Black to Move
(Counterattack)

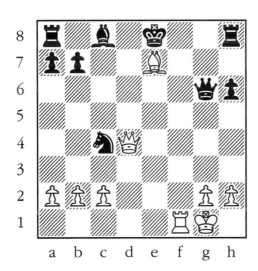

285.
Black to Move
(En Prise)

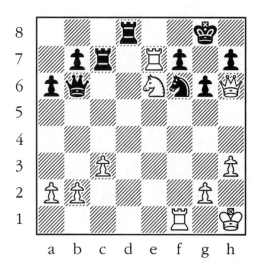

286.
White to Move
(Mating Attack)

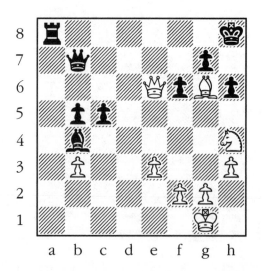

287.
Black to Move
(Fork)

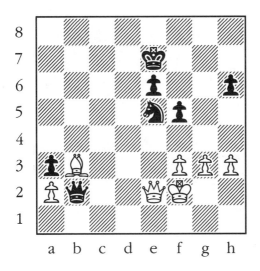

288.
White to Move
(Discovery)

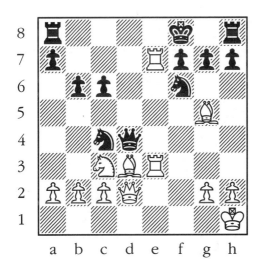

289.
White to Move
(Pin)

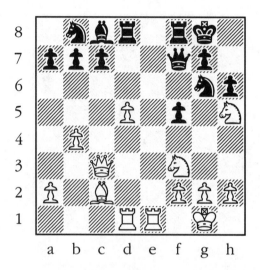

290.
White to Move
(Promotion)

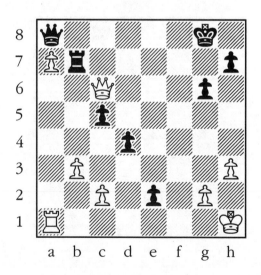

291.
White to Move
(Back Rank)

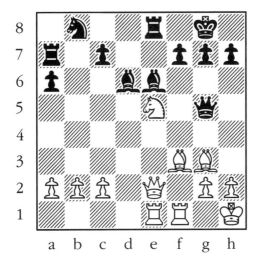

292.
White to Move
(Simplification)

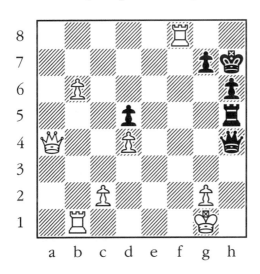

293.
White to Move
(Deflection)

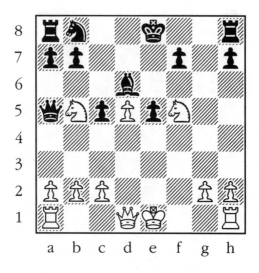

294.
White to Move
(Untrapping)

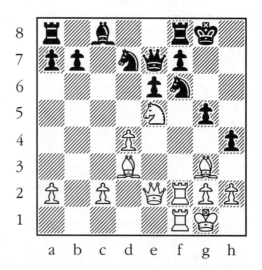

295.
White to Move
(En Prise)

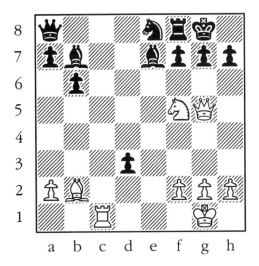

296.
Black to Move
(Mating Attack)

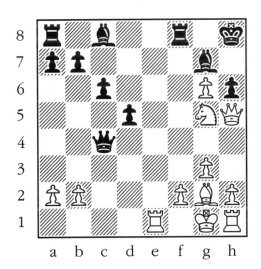

297.
Black to Move
(Fork)

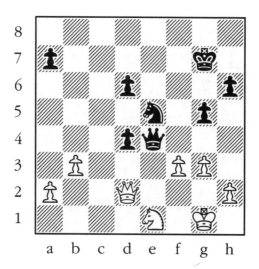

298.
Black to Move
(Removing the Guard)

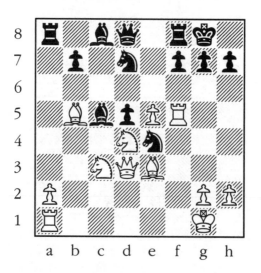

299.
White to Move
(Promotion)

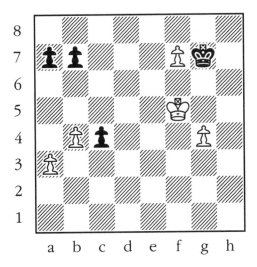

300.
Black to Move
(Driving Off)

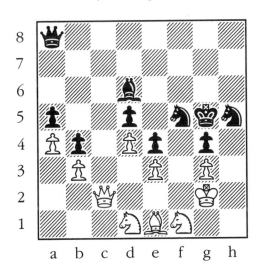

301.
White to Move
(Stop Promotion)

302.
White to Move
(Skewer)

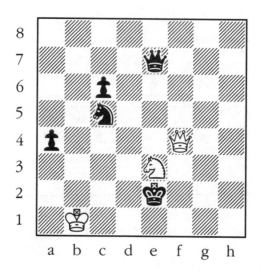

303.
White to Move
(Stop Promotion)

SOLUTIONS

#1   **1. Rg4 hxg4; 2. Rxg4** *and mate is unavoidable. For example,* **2...Qb7+; 3. Kg1 f5; 4. Qf6+ Qg7; 5. Qxg7#.**

#2   **1...Qxg3+; 2. hxg3 Rh1#.**

#3   **1...Rf1#.** *That's why you double your rooks.*

#4   **1. Nb6+ Nxb6; 2. Qd8#.**

#5   **1...Qxa2+; 2. Kxa2 Ra8+** *and mate next move.*

#6   **1. Rxf8+** *and mate next move:* **1...Kxf8; 2. Qh8#;** *or* **1...Rxf8; 2. Qe7#;** *or* **1...Kd7; 2. Qxf7#.**

#7   *After* **1...Qxd1+; 2. Kh2,** *Black must still meet the threat of;* **3.Qf7#. 1...Rxg3+** *works:*
(a) **2. fxg3 Qg2#;**
(b) **2. Kh2 Qxf2+;**
(c) **2. Kh1 Qxd1+.**

#8   **1...d4** *is mate by the lowly pawn.*

#9   **1. Qxh6+ gxh6 (1...Kg8; 2. Qxg7#); 2. Rhxh6#.**

#10   **1. Be6+ Kxe6; 2. Qe8+ Nge7; 3. d5#.**

#11   **1...Rg1+; 2. Kxg1 Rxf1** *double check and mate.*

#12   **1...Qf1+; 2. Ng1 Qxg2#.** *The b2-rook should have stayed on b1.*

#13   **1. Qh6#.**

#14   **1. Bc8** *with* **2. Rh5#.**

#15   **1...Rd1; 2. fxg4 hxg4;** *and* **...Rg1#** *shortly thereafter.*

#16   **1. a5+ Kb5; 2. Bd7#.** *Those killer diagonals.*

#17   **1. Rxg8+ Rxg8; 2. Qe7#.**

#18   **1. Qf5#.**

#19   **1...Rf2+; 2. Kg3 Qg1#.**

#20   *Getting the king is better than taking the queen:* **1. Qd3+ Kc5; 2. Qd4+ Kb5; 3. Qb4#.**

#21   **1. Nh6+ Kh8 (**or **1...Kf8; 2. Rd8#); 2. Qg8#.**

#22   **1. Qxf6+ Rxf6 (**else **Qg7#); 2. Rd8#.**

#23   **1. Re7** *mate. Always try to keep it simple.*

#24   **1...Ba4** *with* **2...Rd1#.**

#25 *Black constructs a mating net by* **1...Be2; 2. Nd7 Na3;** *and* **3...Nc2#.**

#26 *Quick, before Black mates at g2:* **1. Qb7+ Kd7; 2. Nf5#.**

#27 **1. Re8+ (a) 1...Qxe8; 2. Qf6# (b) 1...Bxe8; 2. Qf8[g8]#.**

#28 **1. Bg6** *mate.*

#29 **1. Bc5+ Rxc5; 2. Ng8#.**

#30 *Kings in the center don't live too long:* **1. Qf8+ Qe8; 2. Nf7+ Kd7; 3. Qd6#.**

#31 *Lure the king forward, and you've got him:* **1...Rxh4+; 2. Kxh4 Qg4#.**

#32 *After* **1. Nc6+ Ka8,** *White has the choice of king, queen, or rook. You know what to go for:* **2. Qxc8#.**

#33 **1...Qf3** *is the old snap mate.*

#34 **1...Rg4** *and while* **Rh2** *mate can be delayed, ultimately it is unstoppable.*

#35 **1...Bc3+** *blocks the third rank (no Rd3) and sets up mate after* **2. Ka3 Rgb2** *and* **...R6b3#.**

#36 **1...Bxh2+; 2. Kh1** *(or* **2. Rxh2 Qxh2#); 2...Ng3#.**

#37 **1. Ne8+ Qxe5 (or 1...Kg8; 2. Qg7#); 2. Rf8#.**

#38 **1. Qa8** *mate. Since you're not allowed to take the king, checkmate is the next best thing.*

#39 **1. Nxf7+** *followed by* **2. Qg6#.**

#40 *When both kings are menaced, it's best to be on move:* **1...Rh1+; 2. Kg3 Qh4+; 3. Kg2 Qh2#.**

#41 *The power of the double check is revealed in* **1. Re7+ Kd8; 2. Qe8#.**

#42 **1. Qf8+ Rxf8; 2. Rxf8#.** *The back rank checkmate.*

#43 **1...Nh3+;**
(a) 2. gxh3 Qxf2+;
3. Kh1 Ng3#
(b) 2. Kh2 Nhxf2+;
3. Kg1 Qh1#.

#44 **1. Qxh7+ Kxh7; 2. Bg8+ Kh8; 3. Rh7#.**

#45 **1. Rf8+ Rxf8; 2. Qxe5+** *and mates on g7.*

#46 **1. Bh7+ Kh8 (1...Nxh7; 2. Qxh7#); 2. Nxf7#.**

#47 **1. Bf8** *threatening mate at g7 is instantly decisive.* **1....Rxf8** *gives up a back row mate.*

#48 **1. Ra3+ bxa3; 2. Be1+ Ka6 (2...Ka4; 3. b3#); 3. Bf1#.** *The parallel bishops mate.*

#49 **1...Ng3+; 2. Kh2 Nf1+; 3. Kh1 Qh2+; 4. Nxh2 Ng3#** *is a semi-smother.*

#50 *There's a mate to be had by* **1. Qh8+ Bxh8; 2. Rxh8+ Ke7 (2...Kg7; 3. R1h7#); 3. Re1+ Kd6; 4. Re6#.** *But White, with severe time pressure, played* **1. Be6?** *and after* **1...Rf4,** *his flag fell.*

#51 **1. Qf8+ Rxf8; 2. Rxf8#.** *The old back row mate.*

#52   1. Qxf7+ Rxf7; 2. Ng6 *is mate.*

#53   1. Bc5+ *brings about a queen mate at d8 or e7 very shortly.*

#54   1...Bh2+; 2. Kxh2 Qxf2+; 3. Kh1 Bf3#. *Not taking the bishop doesn't help either:* 2. Kg2 Bf3+; 3. Kh3 Qf1+; 4. Kh4 Qxf2+; 5. Kh3 Qg3#.

#55   1. Rg7+ Kf8 (1...Kh8; 2. Nf7#); 2. Nd7+ Ke8; 3. Nf6+ Kf8 (3...Kd8; 4. Rd7#); 4. g6; *and mate coming up with Rf7.*

#56   1. Qg7+ Kxf4; 2. Qg3#.

#57   1. Nf6+ Bxf6; 2. Rg7+ Kf8; 3. Qf7#.

#58   1...Qd2+; 2. Kb1 Qd1+; 3. Rxd1 Rxd1#.

#59   1...Qxh2+; 2. Kxh2 Rh6+; 3. Kg2 Bh3+; 4. Kh2 (*or* h1) Bf1#.

#60   1...Rh5+; 2. Kg1 Rg7+; 3. Kf1 Rh1+; 4. Kf2 Rg2#. *White can drag it out an extra move by dumping his rook at g6.*

#61   1. Bb5+ Nc6; 2. Nf6#.

#62   1. Bd6+ *when Qh8 mate is unstoppable.*

#63   1. Rf4+ Kd3; 2. Rd1+ Kc2 (*or* 2...Ke3; 3. Rf3#); 3. Rf2#.

#64   1. Nf5+ Bxh4 (1...Kg8; 2. Qh7#); 2. Ng6+ Kg8; 3. Nh6#.

#65   1...Qc3+; 2. Ka4 b5+; 3. Kxb5 Qc4+; 4. Ka5 Bd8+; 5. Qb6 Bxb6#. *Also* 5...axb6 *is mate.*

#66   1...Qxh2+; 2. Rxh2 Rg1#.

#67   1...Rxh2+; 2. Kxh2 Rh8#.

#68   1. Ng5+ Kg8; 2. Rxe8+ Nxe8; 3. Qf8#.

#69   1. Nge6+ Kh6 (1...Kf6; 2. Qg5+ Kf7; 3. Qxg7#); 2. f5+ g5; 3. Bxg5+ (*also* 3. fxg6+); 3...Bxg5; 4. Qxg5#.

#70   1. Qxc5+ *forces mate:* (a) 1...Kd8; 2. Qc7+ Ke8; 3. Qc8+ Ke7; 4. Rf7#; (b) 1...Kd7; 2. Rf7+ Be7 (2...Kd8; 3. Qc7+ Ke8; 4. Qc8#); 2. Rxe7+ Kd8; 4. Qc7#.

#71   1...Rd1+; 2. Rf1 Rxf1 *mate.*

#72   1. Rh8+ Kxh8; 2. Qg8#.

#73   1. Qe6+ *forces checkmate.* 1...Re7 *or* 1...Be7; 2. Nf6#. *And if* 1...Qe7, *then* 2. Nxd6+ Kd8; 3. Qc8#.

#74   1. Qg6+ Qg7; 2. Rf8+ Kxf8; 3. Qe8#.

#75   1. Rxh7+ Kxh7; 2. Bxg6+ Kh8 (2...Kxg6; 3. Qf5#); 3. Bg7+ Nxg7 (3...Kxg7; 4. Qf7+ Kh8; 5. Qh7#); 4. Qh4+ *and queen mates at h7.*

#76   1. Qxh7+ Kxg5; 2. Qh4# *or* 2. Qxg6#.

#77   1...Rd1+; 2. Rxd1 Qxd1#. *Start with* 1...Qd1+ *if you're feeling brilliant.*

#78   *There's a straightforward mate by* 1. Qxf7+ Kh8; 2. Qh5+ Kg8; 3. Qh7#.

#79 *Faced with a skewer down the d-file, White's best defense is to attack:*
1. Bxf7+ Kxf7; 2. Ng5+ Ke8 (*or* 2...Kg8; 3. Qe6+); **3. Qe6+ Ne7; 4. Qf7#.**

#80 **1. Rxg7+** *starts a barrage of checks culminating in mate:*
1...Kxg7; 2. Rh7+ Kg8; 3. Bxe6+ Rf7; 4. Bxf7+ Kf8; 5. Ne6+ Ke7; 6. Bg8+ Ke8; 7. Nd6#.

#81 **1. Qh5+ Rh7; 2. Qe8+ Qf8; 3. Qxf8** *mate.*

#82 **1. Rd7+ Kxg6** (1...Kg8; **2. Rg7#**); **2. Rg7** *mate.*

#83 **1. Qg6+ Ke7; 2. Qf7+ Kd6; 3. Nc4** *mate.*

#84 **1. Kg3 g4; 2. Kh4 g5+; 3. Kh5** *and finally* **4. Rf1** *mate.*

#85 **1. Qf8+ Kc7** (1...Ke6[e5]; **2. Qf6#**); **2. Bd8+ Kb8** (2...Kc8; **3. Bb6+ Be8; 4. Qxe8#**); **3. Be7+ Bc8** (3...Kc7; **4. Qd8#**; 3...Be8; **4. Qxe8+ Kc7; 5. Qd8#**); **4. Bd6+ Ka8; 5. Qxc8#.**

#86 **1...Rc2+; 2. Qxc2 Qd4** *mate.*

#87 **1. Qxh6+ Kg8; 2. Qh7#.**

#88 **1. Rd8+ Re8; 2. Rg8+ Kxg8; 3. Rxe8#.**

#89 **1. Rf3+ Kh4; 2. g3+ Kxh3; 3. Qh5+ Qh4; 4. gxh4#.**

#90 **1. Qc5+ Nc6; 2. Qxc6+ bxc6; 3. Ba6+ Kb8; 4. Nxc6#.**

#91 **1. Rxe6+ Nxe6** (1...Kf7; **2. Qg6#**); **2. Qd7#.**

#92 **1. Rf7+ Kg7; 2. Ne7+ Kh8; 3. Rh7#.**

#93 **1. Qa8+ Kc7; 2. Ra7+ Qxa7** (2...Kd6; **3. Qd5#**); **3. Qxa7+ Kd6; 4. Qb6+ Kd7; 5. Qc6#.**

#94 **1...Bd4+; 2. cxd4 Qe3+; 3. Kh1 Qe1+; 4. Nf1 Rxf1+; 5. Qxf1 Qxf1#.**

#95 **1...Nf1+; 2. Rxf1** (**2. Kh1 Rg1#**); **2...Qg3+; 3. Kh1 Qxh3+; 4. Qh2 Qxf1+; 5. Qg1 Qxg1#.**

#96 *You do this in two stages. First* **1. Rc7+ Kf8** (1...Qxc7; **2. Qe8#**); **2. Qxd8+,** *and you've got the queen. Second* **2...Kg7; 3. Rxf7+ Kxf7; 4. Bc4+ d5; 5. Bxd5+ Kg7; 6. Qg8#,** *and you've got the king.*

#97 **1...Ne2+; 2. Rxe2 Rf1+; 3. Kh2 Rh8+; 4. Kg3 Bh4+; 5. Kxg4 Rf4+; 6. Kh3 Bf2#.**
If **2. Kh2** *Black mates by* **2...Rh8+; 3. Rh3 g3+; 4. Kh1 Rf1#.**

#98 *Black strips away the pawn cover so that the heavy pieces can move in:* **1...Rxg3+; 2. Kh2 Rxh3+; 3. Kxh3 Rf3+; 4. Kh2 Qh4+; 5. Kg2 Qg4+; 6. Kh2 Rh3#.**

#99 **1. Qxh7+ Kf7; 2. Nxg5+ Ke8; 3. Qg6+ Kd7; 4. Qe6+ Ke8; 5. Bg6+ Rf7; 6. Bxf7+ Kf8; 7. Nh7#.**

#100 **1. Re1+ Qe5** (1...Kf5; **2. Qe4#**); **2. Rxe5+ dxe5; 3. Qc6+ Kf5** (3...Ke7; **4. Bf6+ Kf8; 5. Qxa8#**); **4. Qf6+ Ke4** (4...Kg4;

5. h3+ Kh5; 6. Qh6#);
5. Qxe5+ Kd3; 6. Qc3+ Ke2
(6...Ke4; 7. Qf3#);
7. Qc2+ Ke1; 8. Bc3#.

#101   1...Qf3 *with* 2...Qh1#
decides. If 2. Kf1, *then*
2...Nh3 *mate.*

#102   1...Be5; *threat* 2...Ra1#. *If*
2. c3; Rd2+ *wins. The same*
goes for 2. Rxe5 fxe5;
3. Kb2 Rd2.

#103   1. f4 *threatens*; 2. Qg5+ Kh7;
3. Qg7# (*or the reverse*).
1...Rg8 *fails against*
2. Qh4+ Kg6; 3. Qg5+ Kh7;
4. Qh5#.

#104   *Both kings are on the verge*
of mate, but it's Black's turn.
1...Qxg4+; 2. Kh6
(2. hxg4 Rh1#); 2...Qxh3+;
3. Qh5 Qxd7 *and wins.*

#105   1. f4 *threatens both* 2. f5 *and*
2. g5+. *If* 1...Nxf4;
2. Nxf4 exf4; 3. Qb2 *is mate.*
One way or another, White
wins a piece.

#106   1...e4 *wins bishop or knight.*

#107   1. Qe5+ *forces Black to part*
with his rook.

#108   1. Qxg7+ *followed by*
2. Qh7+ *picks off the e4*
knight.

#109   1. g7 Kxg7; 2. Nf5+; *and*
3. Nxh4 *confiscates the*
bishop.

#110   1...Qxe5; 2. Qxe5 Bxe5+;
and 3...Bxc7 *lifts a rook.*

#111   1...Qd5+ *wins the white rook.*

#112   *After* 1. axb8/Q+ Kxb8,
White still has to contend
with Black's pawns. So the
simplest way is to pile up on
the pinned bishop:
1. Rf8 *threatening*
2. axb8/Q#.

#113   1...Rxf4; 2. Rxf4 g5 *adds to*
Black's material advantage.

#114   1. Qxc7; *and if* 1...Nxc7;
2. Rxf8+ Qg8; 3. Nf7#.

#115   1. Rxe5 *puts White a rook*
ahead. If 1...Nxe5 (1...Rd1+;
2. Re1+); 2. Bxe5 *and*
3. Bxd6.

#116   *First a skewer on the king and*
knight: 1...Rh8+; 2. Kg2
(2. Rh3 Rxh3+;
3. Kxh3 Qxh1+) Qxh1+;
3. Kf2. *Then a skewer on the*
king and queen: 3...Rh2+;
4. Rg2 Qxg2+. *But don't take*
the queen; go for mate.

#117   1. Ra1 Qxb4; 2. Rxa6.

#118 . *Not* 1...Rb8? 2. c4 Ke7;
3. b3 *and White keeps the*
extra pawn. Correct is
1...Bxb5; 2. Kxb5 Rb8+;
and 3...Rxb2, *maintaining*
equality.

#119   1. Qa3+ Re7; 2. Ba6 *and*
Black can fold his hand.

#120   1...Bxf3; 2. Nxf3 Rxb3.

#121   1. Nxf6+ *discovers on the*
queen.

#122   *Already a piece up, Black*
wins another with 1...Nxd5
discovering on the queen
(2. exd5? Bxg5).

#123   1...Ng4+; 2. hxg4 Qxc6.

#124   **1. Rxf6** *threatens* **2. Rf8#** *as well as* **2. Rf2+.** *If* **1...Kg8; 2. Rg7+** *mates next move. Black can give rook check at a2 but after* **2. Kb1** *he's out of reasonable moves.*

#125   **1...Nc6; 2. Rxb8 Rxb8; 3. Qxb8+** **(3. Bb2 Qb3) Nxb8; 3. Bxe7 Nc6** *leaves Black up material. The same goes for* **2. Bxe7 Rxb3** *and* **2. R1c3 Qxa3.**

#126   **1...Kg7** *and the rook has no way out.*

#127   **1...Qb6** *confiscates the loose rook.*

#128   **1. Nd5** *wins the exchange* (**1...Rec7; 2. Nxc7**) *since* **1...Rxe6** *gets skewered by* **2. Re1.**

#129   *White's rook is hung up to dry after* **1...Bc5+; 2. Ke2 Nc7.**

#130   **1. Nc4 Qb5; 2. Nd6+;** *and* **3. Bxb5** *wins the queen.*

#131   **1...Bxf3** *and* **2...Qxh2+** *wins a pawn.*

#132   **1. Rxd7+ Bxd7; 2. Qxb6+.**

#133   **1...Rxe2; 2. Qxe2 Qc3#.**

#134   **1...Rxf6** *knocks the props out from under white's queen.*

#135   **1. Nxf7 Rxf7; 2. Qxe6** *recovers the sacrificed material with interest. If* **1...Qe8,** *then* **2. Ng5** *and e6 falls.*

#136   **1. g7** *with* **2. g8/Q** *to follow puts an end to Black's resistance.*

#137   **1...Rb7** *and* **2...Rb1** *insures promotion. There's also the slightly longer* **1...Rf2; 2...Rd2;** *and* **3...Rd1.**

#138   **1...Qxc1; 2. Bxc1 h2;** *and* **3...h1/Q.**

#139   **1...Qg4+; 2. Qxg4 hxg4+; 3. Kxg4 Be3; 4. Kf3 Bh6; 5. Ke2 c2;** *and* **6...c1/Q.**

#140   *If* **1. Be7+ Kxe7** (**1...Rxe7; 2. c8/Q**); **2. c/8Q+** (*discovered check!*). *So* **1...Kf5; 2. Bd8 Bxc7; 3. Bxc7** *and White will win.*

#141   **1...Ne5; 2. Rd1** (*else the exchange is lost*). **2...Nxc3** *wins a pawn for a start.*

#142   **1. g3 Rxh2; 2. Rxc4** *leaves White a knight ahead.*

#143   **1...d4; 2. Rc4 Na6;** *and Black wins either knight or bishop.*

#144   **1. axb5 axb5** (**1...Rxb5; 2. Ba4 Rb6; 3. d5**); **2. d5** *winning knight or bishop.*

#145   *Already a pawn up, Black wins another by* **1...h5; 2. Qg5 Qe4+; 3. Be3 Qxf5.** *He can answer:* **4. Qd8+** *with* **4...Bf8;** *and* **5. Qc8** *with* **5...Qd5.**

#146   **1. Bxc5 dxc5; 2. Nxe5** *snipes a pawn.*

#147   **1...Rxg2+; 2. Kxg2 Qxe3.**

#148 *The White knight has too many tasks. The proof:* **1...Qa5+; 2. Nc3 Nxd4.**

#149 **1. Nxf6+ Bxf6; 2. Bxf6** *wins a piece.*

#150 **1. Rxd3 Qxd3 (1...Rxd3; 2. Qxa8+); 2. Re8+ Kh7 (2...Rxe8; 3. Qxd3); 3. Qxd3+ Rxd3; 4. Rxa8.**

#151 **1. Qc6** *threatens* **2. Qe8+ Kg7; 3. Ne6+ Kh6; 4. Qf8#. 1...Kg7; 2. Qe8 Qd6; 3. Ne6+ Kh6.** *Black has managed to cover f8, but after* **4. Qf7** *there's no adequate defense to* **5. Qg7#.**

#152 **1...Rxh2+; 2. Kxh2 Rh8+; 3. Nh5 Rxh5+; 4. Kg3 Nh3+;** *and if White wants to get it over with, then* **5. Kg4 Rh4#.**

#153 *Open and exploit the h-file by* **1. Qg7+ Qxg7; 2. hxg7 Kxg7 (2...Rxf4; 3. Rxh7** with **4. Rh8+); 3. Rxh7+ Kg8 (3...Kf6; 4. Rc7** with **5. Nh7#); 4. Rdh1.** *The threats include* **5. R1h6 Rf6; 6. e5;** *also* **5. Rh8+ Kg7; 6. R1h7+ Kf6; 7. Rxf8+ Rxf8; 8. Rc7;** *and* **9. Nh7#.**

#154 **1...Raf8; 2. Bxd7 Rg2#.** *If* **2. Rh2 Rxh2; 3. Bxd7 Rff2** *with* **4...Rfg2+; 5. Kf1 Rh1#.**

#155 *Black's pieces are scattered and his king exposed. The way to take advantage is by* **1. Rxd5 exd5; 2. Qd6+ Ke8 (2...Kf7[g8]; 3. Qxd5+); 3. e6 Rd8 (if 3...Rf1+; 4. Ke2 Rxc1; 5. Qxd7+ Kf8; 6. Qf7#;** *also*

3...dxe6 *fails to* **4. Qc6+ and 5. Qxa8); 4. Ba3 Bf8; 5. e7** *and wins.*

#156 **1...Bxa6; 2. Qxa6 Bc5+ (2...Nb4; 3. Rxc8); 3. Kf1 Nb4** *gains the exchange.*

#157 **1. Ne4** *gains a knight after* **1...Nd7; 2. Nxg5 Nxe5; 3. dxe5 Rxg6; 4. h4.** *True, at the end, white's knight is hung up on g5, but Black cannot win it, and in the end material superiority must tell.*

#158 **1. Ncxe6 fxe6; 2. Rxg7+ Kh8 (2...Kxg7; 3. Nxe6+); 3. Rxa7** *confiscating two pawns.*

#159 **1. Rh8+ Bxh8; 2. Rxh8+ Kxh8; 3. Nxf7+;** *and* **4. Nxd6.**

#160 **1...Rxe3; 2. Qxe3 Nb3** *hits both rooks and the knight. After* **3. Nf5 Qxe3+; 4. Nxe3 Bxb2** *provides yet a second fork.*

#161 **1...Rgg3** *with the idea of* **2. Rg1 Rxh2+; 3. Qxh2 Rh3** *pinning and winning the queen. Note that* **4. Rg2** *fails against* **4...Qe1+.** *It would also fail even in the event of* **4...Rxh2+; 5. Rxh2 Qxh2+; 6. Kxh2** *because of* **6...bxc3; 7. bxc3 a5;** *followed by* **8...a4** *etc.*

#162 **1. Rxd8? Bxd8; 2. Rxd8 Qe1+** *is a perpetual. So first* **1. Qf2+** *and if* **1...Ke8; 2. Rxd8+ Bxd8; 3. Re1** *winning the queen.*

#163 1...Re1; 2. Kf3 Qf8+;
3. Qf4 (3. Kg2 Qf1#);
3...Rf1+ *finishing with a
skewer. The same would
happen after 3. Nf6+ Qxf6;
4. Qxf6 Rf1+. Yet another
option, perhaps simpler, is
2...Rf7+.*

#164 1...Rxb3+; 2. cxb3
(2. Nxb3 Qxf2); 2...Qxc1+;
3. Ka2 Qa3+; 4. Kb1 Rc1#.

#165 *The play is against the pinned
d7 rook:* 1. e6 Rd2+;
2. Kd1 Rd1+; 3. Rxd1 Rxb7.
*Black has succeeded in
breaking the pin but now the
rook falls vulnerable to a new
tactic:* 4. Rd7+ Rxd7;
5. exd7 *and promotes.*

#166 1. Rxc8 Rxc8; 2. Bxf5 *snares
the rook. If* 2...Qxf5; 3. Ne7+
while 2...Rc1+;
3. Qxc1 Qxd5 *drops the
queen to* 4. Qc8+ *and*
5. Be6+.

#167 1...Nxe3; 2. fxe3 Qxe3+;
followed by 3...Rxc3 *and
4...Rxc1. On* 2. Qe2 Ng4! *is
sufficient to keep the pawn.*

#168 1. Rc1 Qxa3; 2. Rxc8+ Kd7;
3. Rc7+ *and* 4. bxa3 *wins a
rook.*

#169 1...Ra3; 2. Ke2 (*or* Kc2)
2...Ra1 (*threat to queen*);
3. Rxh2 Ra2+; *and*
4...Rxh2.

#170 1. Bd5 Qf6; 2. R1c7 *wins
a piece as there is no
convenient way to save the d7
knight. If it moves, then* Rxe7;
and on 2...Nhf8; *comes* 3. g5
hxg5; 4. Bxg5 *trapping the
queen.*

#171 1...Rxg2+; 2. Kxg2 Nf4+;
and 3...Nxd3.

#172 1. Nxe6; *and if* 1...Bxe6;
2. Qxh6+ Kg8; 3. Qxg7#.

#173 1...Rg4; 2. Rxb6 Rxg3+;
3. Kf2 Ra3 *winning the a2
pawn.*

#174 *White has just played 1. e6
discovering on the h8 rook.*
1...Nd3+; 2. Rhxd3 (*if*
2. Qxd3 Bxe6; 3. Re3 Bf5);
2...Qxd4; 3. Rxd4 fxe6 *with
an extra pawn for Black.*

#175 1...Nd5 *unmasks the f-file for
attack. Hopeless is*
2. exd5 Qxf2# *or*
2. Rxf7+ Rxf7+;
3. Ke2 Rf2+. *That leaves*
2. Qe2 2...Ne3+;
3. Ke1 Qg1+; 4. Kd2 Rxf2+.

#176 1...Nd4 *and the queen has no
safe square. The best chance
is* 2. Rxd4 Bxd5; 3. Rxd5;
*with rook and bishop for the
queen.*

#177 1...h5; 2. Qf4 Ne2+; *and*
3...Nxf4 *wins the queen.*

#178 1...Nd5 (*threat* 2...Kxd6)
wins the exchange.

#179 *The white knight is lost after*
1...Kg7; 2. Re8 Bd7;
3. Rd8 Nf8; *and* 5...Kxg8.

#180 1...Rc7 (*threat* 2...Rb6);
2. a5 Rb5 (*threat* 3...Rxa5);
3. Ra1 Rbc5; *and there's
nothing to be done about
4...R5c6 catching the queen.*

#181 1...Nxa3; 2. Bxa3 Bxa3;
*followed by ...Rxa5 puts
Black a pawn ahead.*

#182 *White clears the air and wins a pawn with* **1. Rxf6+ Rxf6; 2. fxg4+ Kg6+; 3. Bxf6 Kxf6.** *Then Black cannot deal with* **4. c4; 5. c5;** *and* **6. b6;** *producing passed pawns on opposite sides of the board.*

#183 **1...Bxg2; 2. Qxg2 Qxh4+; 3. Kg1 Rg3** *gets the queen.*

#184 **1. Bxh6 gxh6; 2. Bxe6 fxe6; 3. Qg6+;** *and mate next. This is the main line. Black can vary, but he's in trouble no matter what he does.*

#185 **1. Rxe5 Qxe5; 2. Bxg6+ Ke7** (**2...hxg6; 3. Qxg6+** *and* **4. Qf7#**); **3. Nf7 hxg6; 4. Nxh8** *leaves White on top. Another thought is* **1. Bxe6 Bxe6; 2. Nxe6 Qxe6; 3. Qg7** *but it's less convincing.*

#186 *Simplest is* **1...Qxe4+; 2. Bxe4 Bxe4;** *and* **3...b1/Q.**

#187 **1...Bxb3** *clears a path for the c-pawn:* **2. Qxb3** (**2. Qc1 Bd5** *and the b-pawn joins the advance*) **2...c2;** *and* **3...c1/Q.**

#188 **1...a3**
(a) **2. Nxb3 Rxb3;**
3. Rxb3 a2 *and promotes;*
(b) **2. Rxb3 a2;**
3. Rxc3 bxc3; 4. Nb3 c2;
5. Ke3 a1/Q; 6. Nxa1 c1/Q+.

#189 **1. Bd4** *threatens*
2. Bc5+ Ke6; 3. Bb6 Qxb6;
4. d8/Q. *Black can distract with* **1...c3; 2. Bxc3;** *but then White regroups with* **Be1; Bf2; Bc5+;** *etc.*

#190 **1. d8/Q+ Rxd8;**
2. Rxd8 Kxd8 (**2...Rxc5; 3. a7); 3. a7 Ra5; 4. Nb7+;** *and* **5. Nxa5.**

#191 **1...Bd5; 2. Rb6** (*if* **2. Rd3 Bc4** *and* **2. Rb5 Nc3+**) **2...Nxe3; 3. Kxe3 Ra3+** *picks off the f3 knight.*

#192 *It's safe to take* **1...Nxf6.** *True, Black gets driven off,* **2. Rg7+ Kf8; 3. Kxf6;** *but then he does likewise to White's king,* **3...Rf2+.** *Best is to return the piece* **4. Bf3 Rxf3+; 5. Kg6** *and the game should be a draw.*

#193 **1...Re1**
(a) **2. Qxe1 Qxf3+;**
(b) **2. Qf2 Nxe4+;**
(c) **2. Qd3 Rxe4;** *and if* **3. Bxe4? Nxe4+.**

#194 **1. Ne6+ Ke7; 2. Qc7+ Kxe6; 3. Qxf7+;** *and* **4. Qxe8.**

#195 **1. Rd1** *pushes the Black queen from d6 when the White queen enters:*
(a) **1...Qc7; 2. Qe6+ Kh8;**
3. Rd7 Qg3; 4. Bf6+; *etc;*
(b) **1...Rae8; 2. Rxd6 Rxe2;**
3. Rxg6+; *and* **4. Rxc6.**

#196 **1. Qe2 Be6** (**1...Qxe2;**
2. Nxf7#; *also* **1...Re8;**
2. Qxe7 Rxe7; 3. Rg8#);
2. Nxf7+ Qxf7; 3. Qe5+ *and mate next move.*

#197 *Prior to entry Black must first reposition his queen:*
1...Qb4; 2. Kb1 Qa4;
3. Kc1. *That done, he overloads the white queen with* **3...Re8; 4. Qh1 Qa1+;**
5. Kd2 Qxb2+; *etc.*

#198   1...Nxe5; 2. fxe5
(2. gxf6 Nxf3) 2...hxg5;
3. exf6 Bxg3; 4. fxg7 Rhg8;
and ...Rxg7 wins a pawn.

#199   1. Bxf7+ Kf8 (or 1...Kh8;
2. Rd8+ Bf8; 3. Rxf8+);
2. Rd8+ (2...Rxd8;
3. Qxc3 Kxf7; 4. Qc7+);
2...Ke7; 3. Qe6+ Kxd8;
4. Qd6#.

#200   1...Rf8+; 2. Kg1 Qf6;
3. Bc3 Bxe4 *wins a pawn
since* 4. Q(R)xe4 *allows*
4...Qf2+; 5...Qf1+; *and*
6...Rxf1#.

#201   *This is an important position
from the Scotch opening.
White's last move, Bg5 is
a mistake—he should play
1. Nxc6 followed by 2. Bd3
instead. After* 1...h6; 2. Bh4
(*if* 2. Bxf6 Qxf6 *Black has the
advantage of the two bishops
and already stands better*);
2...g5; 3. Nxc6 (3. Bg3 Nxe4
*and White is simply a pawn
down*); 3...bxc6;
4. Bg3 Nxe4; 5. Qd4 Bxc3+;
6. bxc3 0-0. *Black is doing
very well* (7. Qxe4? Re8;
8. Be5 d6.). *Sometimes you
also have to study some
opening theory to become a
stronger player!*

#202   1. Qd7 *with threats of*
2. Qg7# *and* 2. Qxe8+.
1...Nf6; 2. Bxf6 *doesn't
change anything.*

#203   (a) 1...Bb5? 2. Qb4#
(b) 1...Rb5? 2. Qxa7#;
(c) 1...Ka4! and Black goes
on to win.

#204   *A rook down, Black should
resign. He doesn't, so White*
has to persuade him:
1. Nf6+ Kg7; 2. Bxd6.

#205   1. Rg1 g3+; 2. Rxg3 *wins a
pawn for the moment.*

#206   *On the verge of checkmate,
Black escapes by* 1. Qg4+.
After 1...Kxg4 *it's a draw by
stalemate.*

#207   1. Qd7 (*threat* 2. Bxc7) *wins
a piece. If* 1...Qxd7; 2. cxd7
attacking rook and knight.

#208   1...a6 *puts White in
zugzwang. The king has to
back off* 2. Kb2[d2]; *letting
Black's in:* 2...Kb4 *and*
3...Kxa5.

#209   1...Rxf3. *White cannot
recapture.*

#210   1...Bxd4; 2. exd4 Rc4 *wins
a pawn. But not* 2...Rd3?
3. axb5 axb5; 4. Ra5; *and
White can make a draw.*

#211   1...Bxg3+ *enables Black to
save his bishops, if*
2. Kxg3 Nf5+. *While on*
2. Kg2 Bh5 (*but not*
2...Bxc2?; 3. Rd2);
3. Rd7 Bh4. *White should
probably clip the a6 pawn*
(3. Rxa6), *but three minor
pieces normally beat a rook.*

#212   1. Bf5 *unpins the g-pawn.
After Black moves his queen,
there comes* 2. g5 *menacing
the knight and mate on h7.*

#213   1. Be2 *stops Black's threat
of ...Nf3+. In turn White
has two threats of his own:*
2. Bxe7 *and* 2. Bh5. *Black
cannot parry both.*

#214 **1. Rxg6+ hxg6; 2. Qxd2** *puts White two pawns up. It's also an example of a desperado, the lost rook taking some of the enemy down with him.*

#215 **1...Rd1; 2. Qxd1 Nf2+.**

#216 **1...Bxg5; 2. Nxg5 Qd7** *enables Black to keep his head above water. Acceptance of the sacrifice* **1...Rxf7; 2. Rxf7 Kxf7** *yields White too strong an attack after* **3. Qxh7+ Ke8; 4. Bxg6+ Kd7; 5. Nxd5 exd5; 6. Bf5+;** *etc.*

#217 **1...Bf3+; 2.Q[R]xf3 Rg1#.** *If* **2. Nxf3** (*or* **2. Rg2**) *then* **2...Qxf4** *makes off with the queen.*

#218 *After* **1...Rf1+** *White has to part with his knight to save his king:* **2. Nf2 Rxf2+.**

#219 *Black's task is to hang on to his extra piece. First* **1...Bc4** *keeps the bishop by threatening mate at f1. After say* **2. Rf2** *Black has time to move his rook to safety.*

#220 **1...Ba6** *saves the bishop,* (*also* **...Bd3; ...Be2**) *attacks White's at a8, and threatens* **2...Rc1+** *with mate next.*

#221 *White's pieces are swarming but there's no reason to panic. The simple capture* **1...gxf6** *wins the exchange. Then* **2. Bxf6 Qd8!** *collapses the attack.*

#222 **1. Kh2**
(a) **1...Rxe1; 2. Qf3**
(b) **1...Bxe1; 2. Qf4.** *In both cases the attack on f7 allows*

White to regain his piece with advantage.

#223 **1...Qe7** *attacks the bishop while preparing to mate with* **2...Re1+** *etc.*

#224 *White's king can be deflected by* **1...Ra1+; 2. Kxa1 Qxa3+; 3. Kb1 Nxd4** *putting Black way ahead.*

#225 **1. Qc8+ Kg7; 2. Bf3** *evades the fork, keeping a winning material advantage.*

#226 **1...Qg8!** *collapses the enemy attack:*
(a) **2. Rxf6 Nxf6** *or*
(b) **2. Qe7 Qf8; 3. Qxf8+ Nxf8** *etc.*

#227 *Black may have expected a recapture at d3. Instead there comes* **1. Qe5 f6; 2. Qxe6+ Kf8; 3. Bxf6** *or* **2...Kg7; 3. Qxe7+ Qxe7; 4. Rxe7+ Kf8; 5. Rxh7.**

#228 **1. Qf2** *is the only good move, for it keeps the exchange after* **1...Qxf2+; 2. Rxf2.** *Plus it gets the queens off the board.*

#229 **1. Rxb8 Bxd5** *is only an exchange while* **1. Rxe6 Rd8** *gets the piece back. Best is* **1. Be4+ f5; 2. Rxe6+** *coming away with a full piece.*

#230 **1...Nxe4; 2. Nxe4 Re3+;** *and* **3...Rxe4** *wins a pawn.*

#231 *In a bad position you still have to put up resistance. Black played* **1...Bxg5** *losing the bishop after* **2. Rh5.** *Also poor is* **1...Rf8; 2. Qxe7 Rxf3;**

3. Rh8+ Kc7; 4. Qd8+. *So the best is* **1...Bf8** *when* **2. Rh8** *can be answered with* **2...Qb4.**

#232 **1. Qxd5** *lifts a pawn as* **1...Rxd5; 2. Nd7+ Rxd7; 3. Re8+** *gives a back row mate.*

#233 **1...Qf6** *threatens;* **2...Qxf2+; 3. Kd1 Qxf1#;** *as well as the a1-rook.*

#234 **1. d6 Qxd6; 2. Qxb7;** *or* **1...Qg5; 2. Rc3(e1)** *suffices.*

#235 **1...Rxd7? 2. Nxf6+.** *So* **1...Bh4+; 2. g3 Rxd7** *wins the exchange.*

#236 *Sometimes the obvious move is also the best move. Here* **1. cxd4 Rxc2; 2. Rb8** *wins the bishop with check.*

#237 **1...Qxa2** *is safe since* **2. Ra1** *is controlled by* **2...Ne4.**

#238 *The idea is to collect the pinned e4 knight without getting mated. Rule out* **1...fxe4? 2. Qxf7#;** *and go with* **1...Bxe3+; 2. Rxe3 Qe7;** *after which the knight does fall.*

#239 **1...Nf4; 2. Qd2** **(2. Qd1 Nxg2; 3. Kxg2 Bxf3+); 2...Bxf3; 3. gxf3 Qg5** *with a mating attack.*

#240 *White must avoid* **1. Qg8+ Kg6; 2. Bf7+ Kf6; 3. Bxe8 Qxd7.** *So,* **1. Be6 Qxb4; 2. g4 Qxc5; 3. Qg8+ Kg6; 4. Bf5+;** *and mate next move.*

#241 *The important thing is not to panic.* **1...Nxd7? 2. Qxf7#;** *and* **1...Rxd7; 2. Qh8+;** *with* **3. Qxa8** *are both bad for Black. But* **1...Ke7** *recovers the piece, say* **2. Ne4 Nxd7** *when chances are roughly even. Black has two rooks for the queen and it's not so easy to get at his king.*

#242 **1. Bxh7+ Kxh7; 2. Ng5+;** *and* **3. Qxg4.** *That's what can happen when the pinning bishop is unprotected.*

#243 **1. Nxb7** *puts White two pawns up as* **1...Rxb7** *gets mated after* **2. Re8+ Rxe8; 3. Qxe8+;** *etc.*

#244 **1. Rf3** *threatens* **2. Rxf6** *and* **3. Qxh7#;** *also* **2. Nxf7 Rxf7; 3. Re7.** *Having the rook at f3 stops ...Nd5 as a possible defense.*

#245 **1. Qe5+ Kd2; 2. Qc3+ Kd1; 3. Qa1+** *forces a trade of queens after which the h-pawn romps. Other first moves for Black are no better,* **1...Kf3; 2. Qf5+;** *or* **1...Kd3; 2. Qb5+.**

#246 **1. Rd8+ Kh7** (*or* **1...Rxd8; 2. Qxb7); 2. Qxb7 Rxb7; 3. Rxa8** *gains a whole rook.*

#247 *The tempting* **1...Nxd4?** *fails to the in-between-check* **2. Bxd7+ Kxd7; 3. Ne5+;** *so the correct move is* **1...0-0;** *setting up for* **2...Nxd4.**

#248 **1...Qxc7; 2. dxc7 Nxd4** *puts Black two pieces ahead.*

#249 *Behind by a pawn, Black heads for a draw:* **1...Bxg2+;**

2. Kxg2 e5; 3. Rc4
(3. Rf7+ Kg4); 3...exf4;
4. Bxf4. *The ending, rook and
bishop vs. rook (no pawns)
is a theoretical draw, though
the tendency nowadays is to
make Black play it out for fifty
moves and demonstrate the
draw at the board. It's not so
easy to do.*

#250   *It's okay to take the knight,*
1...cxd5. *The attempt to
trap the queen* 2. Bc7 *fails to*
2...Bb4+ *and* 3...Qe7.

#251   1...Qg5 *loses on the spot to*
2. Qe8# 1...Qe7. 2. Ne4 *with*
3. Nf6+ *looks dangerous.
And the check at d4 takes the
queen too far from the king.
That leaves* 1...g6 *and if*
2. Bxg6 *then* 2...Qg5 *kills off
the attack.*

#252   1...g5; 2. Bg3 Nxe4 *wins a
pawn.* 3. Rxe4? Rc1+ *leads
to mate.*

#253   *White's extra rook is useless
as he loses his queen or gets
mated:* 1...Bb6;
2. Qxd5 Qe1+;
3. Bxe1 Rxe1#.

#254   1...Nd3 *threatens rook and
knight. If* 2. Rxd3 exd3;
3. Rxe5 Ra1+; *and* mates.
*Nothing else seems to work,
for if* 2. Ne6 *then simply*
2...Nxe1.

#255   1. Rxe7 Nxe7; 2. Rxe7 Qxe7;
3. Qb8#.

#256   1. Qf5+ Kb8;
2. Qxd5 Qxe1+; 3. Kh2; *and
Black cannot save both king
and queen.*

#257   1. Nxe4 Qxc2; 2. Nxf6+; *and*
3. Bxc2 *wins a piece.*

#258   1...Kb2; 2. Rd1 (2. Nc7,
*giving up the exchange looks
best);* 2...Re6+; 3. Ne3
(3. Kd2 Re2#); 3...dxe3 *wins
a piece.*

#259   *Behind in material, White
does his best to make a draw,
by* 1. Rd8+;
(a) 1...Kf7? 2. Bc4+;
(b) 1...Ke7? 2. Bh4+;
(c) 1...Kg7; 2. Rd7+ Kf8;
3. Rd8+; *etc.*

#260   1...Rxe2 *wins a rook and
precludes* 2. Bxe5 *because
of* 2...Rxg2+; 3. Kh1 Nf2
*forking king and queen. It
also happens to be mate.*

#261   1. Rh3 *with the threat of*
2. Qh8+ Bxh8; 3. Rxh8#
decides. On 1...Rxf6;
2. exf6 Bxf6 *comes* 3. Qh6
with 4. Rdg3.

#262   1...Rxf2 *and if*
2. Qxg4 Rxf1+;
3. Kg2 R8f2+; 4. Kh3 Rh1#.

#263   1. Qxe8+ Rxe8;
2. Rxe8+ Qc8;
3. Rxc8 Kxc8; 4. Rxd5 *wins
the exchange and a pawn.*

#264   1. Qb5 *threatens the bishop
but mainly a back row mate
with* Re8+; *etc. If for example*
1...Qa6 *then* 2. Re8+ Nf8;
3. Qxa6 Bxa6; 4. Rxa8. *No
better is* 1...Ba6;
2. Re8+ Nf8; 3. Rxa8 Bxb5;
4. Rxf8#.

#265   1. Rxe6+ Rxe6;
2. Re8+ Kxe8; 3. Kxe6 *is a
straightforward win in the
king and pawn ending.*

187

#266 1. Bf3+ Rxf3; 2. Rh4+; *and* 3. Kxf3.

#267 1. d6 Re6 (1...cxd6; 2. Bb5+ *and* 3. Bxe8); 2. Bxe6 fxe6; 3. Rf8 *traps the queen.*

#268 1. Kf2 *intending to shuffle the king back and forth between g2 and f2. If* 1...g3+ *then* 2. Kf3; 3. Kg2; *etc. While on* 1...d4, *White has* 2. Nxd4 Bxd4+; 3. Kg3; *and* 4. Kxg4.

#269 *In a pinch* 1. Rxe2 *is good enough, but there's a better version:* 1. Bh7+ Kh8 (1...Kxh7; 2. Qe4+; *and* 3. Qxe2); 2. Rxe2 Qxe2; 3. Qxf7; *and the threat of* 4. Qxg7# *decides.*

#270 1...Bxa3, *since* 2. Nxf6 gxf6; 3. Nf3 Bb4 *recovers the exchange and stays a pawn ahead.*

#271 *The best way out of a difficult situation is* 1...Qc5+; 2. Qxc5 Bxc5+; 3. Kh1 Bxb5; 4. Nxb5 Ke7 (*or* 4...0-0). *Above all, don't take the queen,* 1...Bxc6; 2. Bxc6+ *loses.*

#272 1. Ra7 Bb3; 2. Kd6; *and if* 2...Rxc4; 3. Ra8+ Rc8; 4. b7 *decides.*

#273 1. Rxa2 Rxa2; 2. Rd8+ Bf8; 3. Bh6 *and* Rxf8 *mate.*

#274 1. Nxf6+ gxf6; 2. Qe4; 1...Nxf6; 2. Bxf6 (*better than* 2. Bxh7+ Nxh7; 3. Rxd8 Bxd8 *with rook and bishop for the queen*) *wins a piece, for if* 2...Bxf6; 3. Bxh7+ Kxh7; 4. Rxd8 Rxd8; 5. Qe4+; *and* 6. Qxa8.

#275 1. Qxe4 fxe4; 2. Bxc7 Rxc7; 3. b5; *followed by* Rd1 *is technically the simplest way to win and deserves preference over* 1. Qd7.

#276 *White lifts at least a pawn after* 1. Rxf7 *since Black can't afford* 1...Bxf7? 2. Qa6+ Kb8; 3. Nc6+; *and* 4. Qxa7#. *So Black has to move his queen and he has to be careful:*
(a) 1...Qd6; 2. Ne4; *or*
(b) 1...Qh4; 2. Rxg7 Qxh2; 3. Nf3 *both trap the queen;*
(c) 1...Qg5; 2. Ne4 Qh4; *but then* 3. g3 *along with* 4. Rxg7 *gets a second pawn.*

#277 1. Nd3+ Bxd3; 2. b4+ (*not* 2. Kxd3 Kb4 *and Black penetrates*); 2...Kd5; 3. Kxd3; *and the ending should be drawn.*

#278 *With a big lead in development, White should look to open lines of attack.* 1. Nd5 *threatens the queen as well as* Nc7+. *Black has to take the knight and then try to block the e-file.* 1...exd5; 2. Rhe1 Ne5; 3. Nxe5 Be6. *But the bishop gets undermined by* 4. Nxf7 (*also* 4. Nxg6 fxg6; 5. Qxg6+) *with* 4...Qxf7; 5. Bxg6; *or* 4...Kxf7; 5. Qxg6+; *etc.*

#279 *The only way to hold off* Rh8# *is to give a bunch of checks and hope that something good will happen at the end.* 1...Qf1+; 2. Kh2 Qh1+; 3. Kxh1 Re1+; 4. Kh2 Rh1+; 5. Kxh1 Rh3+; 6. Kg1 Rh1+; 7. Kxh1 *stalemate.*

#280 1...Rd1; 2. h8/Q Rg1+; 3. Kf3 (3. Kh3 Rh1+ *skewers the queen*) 3...Qd1+; 4. Ke3 Re1#.

#281 *White wins by triangulating his king over the squares f4, e4, e5, turning the move over to Black.* **1. Kf4 Ke8** (1...Kf7; 2. Kf5—*Black is trying to avoid this position*); **2. Ke4 Kf8; 3. Ke5.** *Now it's Black to move:* (a) **3...Kf7; 4. Kf5;** *and* **5. Kg6** *winning the h6 pawn;* (b) **3...Ke8; 4. Ke6 Kf8; 5. f7 Kg7; 6. Ke7 Kh7; 7. Kf6** (*not; 7. f8/Q? stalemate*); **7...Kh8; 8. f8/Q+** *and mate next move.*

#282 **1. R1c2?** *fails against* **1...Rcd8; 2. Ke1 Rd1+; 3. Kf2 R8d2.** *The right way is* **1. R3c2! Rcd8; 2. Ke1 Rxc2; 3. Rxc2 Rd3; 4. Rc3;** *and White holds.*

#283 1...Rab8; 2. Qd6 Qxf1+; 3. Kxf1 Rb1+; 4. Ke2 Rc2 *mate.*

#284 1...Kxe7; 2. Qxh8 (2. Re1+ Be6); 2...Bh3 (*also* 2...Qxg2+; 3. Kxg2 Bh3+; 4. Kxh3 Rxh8); 3. Re1+ Kf7; 4. Rf1+ Ke6; 5. Re1+ Kd5; 6. Rd1+ Kc6 *and wins. In the game Black played* 1...Qb6 *but White was still kicking after* 2. Bc5.

#285 *Stay away from* 1...Rxe7? *also* 1...fxe6? *both allowing* 2. Qg7#. *Just defend the threat* 1...Nh5; 2. Rxc7 Ng3+; 3. Kh2 Nxf1+; 4. Kh1 Ng3+; 5. Kh2 Nf5; *and you should be able to take something at the end.*

#286 *The skewer* 1. Be4 *sets up a series of discovered checks for the knight.* 1...Qa6; 2. Ng6+ Kh7; 3. Ne5+ (*had the black queen gone to c8 then* 3. Ne7+); 3...Kh8; 4. Nf7+ Kg8; 5. Nxh6+ (*had the black queen played to b8 then* 5. Nd8+); 5...Kh8; 6. Qg8+ Rxg8; 7. Nf7#.

#287 1...Nd3+; 2. Ke3 Qxe2+; 3. Kxe2 Nc1+; 4. Kd2 Nxb3+; *and if* 5. axb3; a2 *makes a new queen.*

#288 *White has pleasant choices. He can win the queen by* 1. Rxf7+ Kxf7; 2. Bg6+; *and* 3. Qxd4; *or he can stay a piece ahead by* 1. Bxc4 Qxc4. *In this last line* 1...Qxd2; 2. Rxf7+ Kg8; 3. Rxf6+ Qd5; 4. Bxd5+ cxd5; 5. Rd6 *puts White two pieces up.*

#289 1. d6 *threatens both* 2. Bb3 *and* 2. dxc7. *And* 1...cxd6 *is not a defense after* 2. Bb3 d5; 3. Rxd5 Rxd5; 4. Bxd5 Qxd5; 5. Qxg7#.

#290 1. Qxb7 e1/Q+ (1...Qxb7; 2. a8/Q+); 2. Rxe1 Qxb7; 3. Re8+ Kf7; 4. a8/Q.

#291 1 Nxf7 *lifts a pawn for a start. If* 1...Bxf7; 2. Qxe8+ Bxe8; 3. Rxe8+ Bf8 (3...Kf7; 4. Bh5#); 4. Bd5+ Qxd5; 5. Rxf8#.

#292 *Eliminate Black's counterplay and the b-pawn decides:* 1. Rh8+ Kxh8; 2. Qe8+ Kh7; 3. Qxh5 Qxh5; 4. b7; *and* 5. b8/Q.

189

#293   *The idea is to draw the Black queen away from c7 so that after Black saves his bishop, White has Nc7+ winning the rook.* **1. Qd2** *is answered by* **1...Bc7.** *So,* **1. b4 Qxb4+ (1...Qxb5; 2. Nxd6+); 2. c3 Qe4+; 3. Qe2 Qxe2+** (*again* **3...Qxf5; 4. Nxd6+); 4. Kxe2 Be7; 5. Nc7+** *etc.*

#294   *The bishop is untrapped by* **1. Nxd7 Nxd7; 2. Bxh4;** *and if* **2...gxh4; 3. Qg4+ Kh8; 4. Qh5+ Kg7; 5. Qh7#.**

#295   *The best way to take the bishop is* **1. Nh6+ Kh8; 2. Qxe7** *threatening* **3. Qxf8#** (a) **2...Rg8; 3. Nxf7#;** (b) **2...Nf6; 3. Qxf6 gxf6; 4. Bxf6#;** (c) **2...Nc7(d6); 3. Bxg7+ Kxg7; 4. Qg5+ Kh8; 5. Qf6#.**

#296   **1...Bg4; 2. Qh4 Rxf2;** (a) **3. Kxf2 Bd4+; 4. Re3 Qe2+;** (b) **3. Nf7+ Rxf7; 4. gxf7 Bd4+;** (c) **3. h3 Rxg2+; 4. Kxg2 Qc2+; 5. Kf1 Rf8+; 6. Nf7+ Rxf7; 7. gxf7 Qd3+; 8. Kg2 Qf3+;** *and mate shortly.*

#297   **1...Qxe1+; 2. Qxe1 Nxf3+; 3. Kf2 Nxe1; 4. Kxe1 Kf6; 5. Ke2 Ke5; 6. Kd3 g4;** *when the ending is won for Black. After say,* **7. b4 Kd5; 8. a4 h5; 9. a5 a6;** *White's king must give way, allowing Black's to enter at c4.*

#298   **1...Nxc3; 2. Qxc3 Ra3; 3. Qd2 Rxe3; 4. Qxe3 Qb6; 5. Rd1 Qxb5; 6. Nxb5 Bxe3+** *puts Black ahead.*

#299   **1. Ke6 Kf8** (**1...c3; 2. Ke7 c2; 3. f8/Q+); 2. Kf6 c3; 3. g5 c2; 4. g6 c1/Q; 5. g7#.**

#300   *After* **1...Qh8** *the queen breaks in at h3, winning the g3 pawn. For example,* **2. Qc6 Bxg3; 3. Bxg3 Nhxg3; 4. Nxg3 Qh3+;** *followed by* **5...Qxg3+;** *etc.*

#301   *How to deal with the passed a-pawn? You start with* **1. Bf6;** *and after* **1...Kd5; 2. d3 a2; 3. c4+ Kc5** (**3...dxc3; 4. Bxc3**); *you slip in close to the king:* **4. Kb7;** *finishing up with* **4...a1/Q; 5. Be7#.**

#302   **1. Qf1+ Kd2** (*the knight is immune,* **1...Kxe3; 2. Qe1+** *skewers the queen*); **2. Qd1+ Kc3; 3. Qc2+ Kb4** (**3...Kd4** *allows the fork* **4. Nf5+); 4. Qb2+ Nb3** (**4...Ka5** *is mate in two by* **5. Nc4+** *and* **6. Qb6#**); **5. Qa3+** *with win of the queen or else mate after* **5...Kxa3; 6. Nc2#.**

#303   *White needs to get his rook to the e-file with tempo to stop the black pawns. At the same time he has to guard against stalemate. For example:* **1. Bc6+ Kd6; 2. Rd4+ Ke7; 3. Re4+ Kd6; 4. Rxe3 e1/Q; 5. Rxe1** *stalemate. Best is* **1. Bf5+ Kd8; 2. Rd4+ Ke7; 3. Re4+ Kd8;** *and now;* **4. Bd7** *releases the stalemate,* **4...Kxd7; 5. Rxe3.** *So Black queens,* **4...e1/Q.** *But after* **5. Bb5** *he's hard pressed to stop mate at e8.*

GREAT CARDOZA CHESS BOOKS
ADD THESE TO YOUR LIBRARY - ORDER NOW!

303 TRICKY CHECKMATES by Fred Wilson & Bruce Alberston. Both a fascinating challenge and great training tool, these two, three and four move checkmates are great for beginning, intermediate and expert players. Mates are in order of difficulty, from simple to very complex positions. Learn the standard patterns for cornering the king, corridor and support mates, attraction and deflection sacrifices, pins and annihilation, the quiet move, and the dreaded zugzwang. Examples from old classics to the 1990's illustrate a wide range of ideas. 192 pgs. $12.95.

303 TRICKY CHESS TACTICS by Fred Wilson & Bruce Alberston. This is not just a challenging collection of two and three move tactical surprises for the advanced beginner, intermediate, and expert player—it's also a great training tool! Tactics are presented in order of difficulty so that players can advance from the simple to the complex positions. The examples, from actual games, illustrate a wide range of chess tactics from old classics right up to today. Great stuff! 192 pgs. $12.95.

CHESS ENDGAME QUIZ by Larry Evans. This book features 200 challenges in the multiple choice format. These instructive, elegant and entertaining positions will not only challenge and entertain you but teach you how to improve your engame while trying to find the best move of the three choices presented. Sections include king and pawn endings, minor piece endings, queen endings, rook and pawn endings so you can concentrate on specific areas. What is the best move? Take the plunge and find out! 304 pgs. $14.95

COMPLETE DEFENSE TO KING PAWN OPENINGS by Eric Schiller. Learn a complete defensive system against 1.e4. This powerful repertoire not only limits White's ability to obtain any significant opening advantage but allows Black to adopt the flexible Caro-Kann formation, the favorite weapon of many of the greatest chess players. All White's options are explained in detail, and a plan is given for Black to combat them all. Analysis is up-to-date and backed by examples drawn from games of top stars. Detailed index lets you follow the opening from the point of a specific player, or through its history. 240 pages, $16.95.

HYPERMODERN OPENING REPERTOIRE FOR WHITE by Eric Schiller. This complete opening repertoire for White shows how to stun opponents by "allowing" Black to occupy the center with its pawns, while building a crushing phalanx from the flanks, ready to smash the center apart with Black's slightest mistake. White's approach is easy to learn because White almost always develops pieces in the same manner, but can be used against all defenses no matter what Black plays! Diagrams and explanations illustrate every concept. The Réti and English openings, which form the basis of the Hypermodern, lead to lively games with brilliant sacrifices and subtle maneuvering. 304 pgs, $16.95

GREAT CARDOZA CHESS BOOKS
ADD THESE TO YOUR LIBRARY - ORDER NOW!

10 MOST COMMON CHESS MISTAKES AND HOW TO FIX THEM by Larry Evans. This fascinating collection of 218 errors, oversights, and outright blunders, not only shows the price great players pay for violating basic principles but how to avoid these mistakes in your own game. You'll be challenged to choose between two moves, the right one or the one actually played. From neglecting development, king safety, misjudging threats and premature attacks, to impulsiveness, snatching pawns, and basic inattention, you receive a complete course in where you can go wrong and how to fix it. 256 pgs, $14.95.

100 AWESOME CHESS MOVES By Eric Schiller. This collection of brilliant ideas from real tournaments are not just combinations or tactical swindles, but moves of stunning originality. Schiller has selected 100 awesome moves, and through game positions, examples, and clearly explained concepts, shows players how to improve their grasp of deep positional understandings and swashbuckling tactics. Readers learn how to reinforce their gut instincts to not just reach for the best move, but the inspired move. 288 pages, $18.95.

WINNING CHESS OPENINGS by Bill Robertie. Shows concepts and best opening moves of more than 25 openings from Black's and White's perspectives: King's Gambit, Center Game, Scotch Game, Giucco Piano, Vienna Game, Bishop's Opening, Ruy Lopez, French, Caro-Kann, Sicilian, Alekhine, Pirc, Modern, Queen's Gambit, Nimzo-Indian, Queen's Indian, Dutch, King's Indian, Benoni, English, Bird's, Reti's, and King's Indian Attack. Examples from 25 grandmasters and champions. 144 pages, $9.95

GAMBIT CHESS OPENINGS (GCO) by Eric Schiller. Gambits, where one side sacrifices material for an advance in development, are the most exciting and popular openings in chess! GCO presents every important gambit opening and variation ever played and currently in vogue – more than 2,000 opening strategies in all! Each gambit is covered in detail with a diagram showing the standard position representative of the gambit, the move orders taken to reach there, and an explanation in plain language of the thinking behind the moves. More than 100 complete games are included so that you can see how the ideas behind the gambit are influential all the way through a game. 784 pgs, $24.95.

STANDARD CHESS OPENINGS (SCO) by Eric Schiller. This comprehensive guide covers every important chess opening and variation ever played and currently in vogue. In all, more than 3,000 opening strategies are presented! Differing from previous opening books which rely almost exclusively on bare notation, SCO features substantial discussion and analysis on each opening so that you learn and understand the concepts behind them. Includes more than 250 completely annotated games (including a game representative of each major opening) and more than 1,000 diagrams! This is the standard reference book necessary for competitive play. A must have for chess players!!! 768 pgs, $24.95